How I Became Father to
1000 Children

D1603652

How I Became Father to 1000 Children

And the Life Lessons I Learned

by

Dr. John S. Niles

From the New White Knight Series:

A Better Way of Living

White Knight Publications
Toronto Canada

Published in 2005 by White Knight Publications,
a division of Bill Belfontaine Ltd.
Suite 103, One Benvenuto Place
Toronto Ontario Canada M4V 2L1
T. 416-925-6458 F. 416-925-4165
E-mail: whitekn@istar.ca
Web site: www.whiteknightpub.com

Ordering information

CANADA	UNITED STATES
Hushion House Publishing Inc.	Hushion House Publishing Inc.
c/o Georgetown Terminal Warehouses	c/o Stackpole Distribution
34 Armstrong Avenue,	7253 Grayson Road
Georgetown ON, L7G 4R9	Harrisburg PA, 17111 USA
T: 1-866-485-5556 F: 1-866-485-6665	T: 1-888-408-0301 F: 1-717-564-8307

National Library of Canada Cataloguing in Publication
Niles, John S., 1962-
How I became father to 1000 children / John S. Niles.

ISBN 0-9734186-2-1
1. Child welfare--Canada. 2. Child abuse--Canada.
3. Children's rights--Canada. I. Title.
BX9883.N45A3 2004   362.7'0971   C2004-907131-9

Cover and text design: Karen Petherick, *Intuitive Design International Ltd.*
Typeset in: Times Roman
Editing: Bill Belfontaine
Cover photos: © Firstlight Associated Photographers, Karen Petherick, John Niles

Printed and bound in Canada

I dedicate this book to my wife Liane, who I loved from the first moment I saw her across a crowded classroom, and in whose eyes I saw our children before they were born, and whose voice still makes my heart beat fast whenever I hear it, and whose arms always feel like home.

And to our five children, Sarah, Alyssa, Nathanael, Aaron, and Tabitha. You have been God's greatest gift to us, and you are God's gift to the world. We love you; so live, love, learn and leave behind a lasting legacy of hope for others.

And to the nearly thousand children we have cared for and thousands of children who have yet to find a safe place to belong; may this be the year they become loved and fulfilled.

And finally, I dedicate this work to the Glory of God.

ACKNOWLEDGEMENTS

Whenever I have read books in the past, I skipped reading the acknowledgements. I regret that now, after considering all the people who have contributed to me becoming the person I am today and the prospect of acknowledging them here. They can become more important than the book itself. For the acknowledgements tell of the author's life journey and of the mentors, influencers, leaders and fellow travellers who have come to accompany and help the author along the way in his journey of becoming.

I would like to thank numerous people: first my wife Liane who always encourages me in every new endeavour; our dear friends Rev. Steve and Lynn Davis – your friendship means more than you know; my friends and fellow authors, Bart Mindszenthy and Michael Coren who offered encouragement and help; and to my mentor and friend Dr. Jim Wetheral who always has a wise and witty word at the right time – thank you all.

I would also like to express my appreciation to David Edmison of the Empire Club of Canada, its President, and past Presidents and directors who honoured Liane and me with the Empire Club of Canada's first humanitarian "Community Service Award."

How remiss would I be if I didn't thank Steven LeDrew the past President of the Liberal Party of Canada, and the firm of

LeDrew Laishley, Reed L.L.P., and especially Sylvia Sauros who helped Kits for Kids to become airborne and useful; and Erika Heller, the Community Investment Coordinator of the Hudson's Bay Company and the corporation itself for their support of Kits for Kids by providing the bags for the products to be in.

Thank-you to the church families I have served as minister over the last twenty years, first as a neophyte student minister at Current River United in Thunder Bay, and the Carmen Pastoral Charge in Carmen, Manitoba; then as a newly ordained minister at the Matilda Pastoral Charge near Ottawa, Victoria Park United in Toronto and to St. Andrews United, Markham. You will never know how grateful I am to all for what I have learned from you and with you. It has been such privilege to serve in each pastorate.

And for Karen Petherick's creative work at Intuitive Design International Ltd. Her inspired work speaks for itself when you hold this book in your hands. And to my publisher, editor, writing mentor and friend Bill Belfontaine; thank-you for the many hours of editing, and advice. I learned a long time ago that the editor is always right, expect when he or she is wrong. And Bill was never wrong. For as Stephen King said, "To write is human, to edit divine." And you Bill are divine. Thank-you for believing in me as an author. You are truly the White Knight with your publishing company.

CONTENTS

"Honey, what were you thinking?"

A few years ago, I gave my wife a new licence plate for her van that read 5KIDZ, causing many strange stares and even stranger comments.

Liane was stopped at a red light when the driver of the next car motioned to roll down her window. She did and he asked, "Is that licence plate for real?"

Liane said, "Yes, and what's worse is we've had two more since I got the plate."

The man replied with a confused look on his face, "Honey, what were you thinking? You must have an extremely active husband!"

To which she replied "You don't know the half of it."

After recounting the story when she got home she said, "I didn't have the heart or the time to tell him that those were only seven of the nearly thousand kids we've cared for in our own home."

What were we thinking to undertake such responsibility? I'm not sure except that perhaps we chose to lead a life fifteen years ago that could make a difference in a real and tangible way in the life of disadvantaged children who were scarred physically and emotionally. We knew of the need and felt it was our destiny to decide to fill it. We understood that no one was willing to be available on the basis of twenty-four hours, 365 days a year as an "emergency home" that would take in infants and toddlers who were abandoned, abused or addicted. After looking into the eyes of our children today we remember that it didn't take very long for us to decide what to do.

Since that time *our* eyes have been opened wide. We have seen and cared for children with broken arms, and cracked skulls; babies going through drug and /or alcohol withdrawal brought to our door by social workers at three in the morning before the addicted mother could take the child and escape from the hospital into the night. We have greeted police arriving at our door with an infant found abandoned in a raid on a crack house, and a toddler wandering alone on the street.

As I sit writing this, I have a fourteen-month-old crawling round my feet and her four-year-old brother slopping his breakfast cereal on my laptop while he sits beside me at the kitchen table. James and Julia arrived after we received a call the prior evening. Their sixteen-and-a-half-year-old mother had had enough. If you haven't already done the math, it means she became pregnant the first time at eleven. She is now pregnant with her third. She had been abandoned by her family and also all three fathers of her children.

The reality for these children is pain followed by loss. The certainty was that we would offer them the opposite – a place of healing, love and hope.

Far too much despair, division, and distress inhabit our world; too many live lives of raging, stumbling desperation. What we must do is hold fast to the valuable remark of Bishop Desmond Tutu, "My humanity is bound up in yours, for we can only be human together."

Three men of Africa were asked: "How can you tell when night ends and day begins?"

The first man responds: "When I can distinguish the olive trees from the fig trees, then I know that night is over and day has begun."

The second answers: "When I can see the forms of the animals across the Serengeti, I know that the darkness is ending and the light has come."

Then a man known for his great wisdom said: "When we see a black woman and a white woman and call them both sister, when we see a poor man and a rich man and call them both brother, then the darkness of night has left and the light of day has come."

Each child is welcomed into our home as if they were our own. It may appear strange when we go shopping. Then people see a family with two white parents, a few white children, one is Jamaican, and others who are Native, Asian, Sudanese or East Indian. We are an interesting sight to behold if not a confusing one to many observers.

Echoes from the Past

Answering the phone call from the social workers for James and Julia was an echo of the different kinds of calls I had received on other occasions. The first kind is the call to care for children in crisis. I have received this type of call most of my life. Perhaps, it was out of a subconscious need to respond to the pain that was written large on my father's shattered heart and shown in the agony on his face whenever he spoke of how he and his brother had been abandoned when they were six and eight years old by his adult brothers and sisters and put in one of the last orphanages in Toronto after both their parents died unexpectedly. Though he spoke well of the orphanage, it was cold, sterile, continually smelling of disinfectant, and bereft of that warmth called love. They anguished over the abandonment, and aching hunger for a family was evident with every remembrance of that time. He would continually run away, not necessarily sure where he was going, but desperately looking for some place to belong.

This coupled with my own struggles growing up as a child labelled as one who was "developmentally delayed" caused me to want to make a difference in the lives of children who didn't have the benefit of family who believed in them and where there was a sense of security and love.

The second "call" was a call of God into the ministry. I thought at the time that it would mean that I would leave behind the work that Liane (my wife) and I had both been trained to do. Little did I know that it was but the beginning of something far better and richly fulfilling. We would be called to open our home to hundreds and hundreds of children and to provide the love, security, care and compassion that these little ones might never have experienced. It would mean that we would be called to show God's grace, mercy and love to the abandoned, abused and the forsaken just as Jesus had done in his own way for us.

Living on Purpose

This book is about hope and healing. About lessons learned and lived. About how each and every one of us can make a difference in the lives of our own children and in the world.

Many people have let their lives slide into going through the motions of living. They get up in the morning, have their coffee, go to work and come home. They eat supper, watch TV and then go to bed, only to stumble through the boredom of doing it all over again the next day. They do this day in and day out until they die. Yet, deep within each one who accepts their life this way there is dis-ease; there remains the question, "Is this all there is?" Let me assure you that there is more, much more. You have only to reach out your hand to assist.

I'm convinced that each of us truly wants to make a difference in the world. Yet, many don't know or understand how to tune into doing it throughout their social lives and chosen careers. When you want to achieve meaning, satisfaction, and fulfillment, it is really dependent on how you use your gifts, abilities, talents, time and temperament.

Just what is it that you are after? That question haunted me for years. During college I found the answer in the ideals of being involved in social justice activity and peace marches. For a time that satisfied my longing to make a difference. Later, as a newly graduated social worker filled with idealism I thought, if only I could change one life for the betterment of society then everything I was doing would be worthwhile. However, the pressure to perform to a senseless regimen, the seemingly endless paper work and the manipulation of the bureaucracy interfered with that on a daily basis. Later, I thought it was to be found in obtaining more knowledge through more university degrees and a prominent position in my chosen profession. After achieving a measure of that, I discovered that this still couldn't answer the question satisfactorily. Still later, I changed direction as I sought spiritual insight and found fulfillment in faith. However, I saw that for too many (including myself) the focus was on being so "heavenly minded, that they were of no earthly good." All the while, we continued to receive needy children into our own home daily.

Was I just getting older and less enamoured with the need for the recognition that comes with the achievement of power, position or possessions? Or was I finally beginning to see that the work that we were doing "on the side" with abused children, because we loved them, was more meaningful than many of the other things that demanded our attention?

I have often spoken at various organizations about our work with children needing a break and was astonished when people became overwhelmed. During seminars, speaking engagements and church services there would be a great amount of laughter shared, but often tears fell as I spoke of the challenges of the children, and the lessons we learned. People approached me and said, "You have an amazing ministry here." I was again surprised. I never thought of it as anything special. It was just something we did because we wanted that type of life. We did not see it as anything significant or out of the ordinary. It was then that everything came together. The preverbal light went on and I understood that the call had been answered.

This work has afforded me the opportunity to learn the life lessons needed to experience a life of abundance, significance and substance. I offer you just a few of these lessons as a means of gratitude for all I have been given. These are the things I've learned:

You can *make a difference*
Build a life not a résumé
Everyone needs to know that they belong
What you mess up in life— clean up
Share and care
Flush and wash; cleanliness is next to godliness
Floss
Say, "Please" and "Thank-you"
Say, "I'm sorry"
Pray
Believe there are no failures – only lessons
Everyone needs a nap
Believe it is a wonderful world
I can be anything I want to be
If I stand for nothing, I will fall for anything
When you cross the road, hold hands, and look both ways
It really doesn't take much to make a difference;
        live, learn, love
Leave behind a lasting legacy

For me, our work was not all that amazing. It was simply something we did and did with love and willingness. However, after the Lieutenant Governor of Ontario the Honourable Hilary Weston presented us with the Humanitarian of the Year Award from the Empire Club of Canada, I realized that there was something more to this affair of the heart than I first thought.

This book is the result of that realization.

A Litany of Love

How do you determine the dimensions of devotion? How do you measure the breadth, depth, height and length of love? For those who would wish to know, perhaps this is one way it's been measured, statistically, over the last twelve years:

49,150	Extra meals and bottle feedings
24,350	Changes of cloths, sleepers, booties and socks
21,000	Extra loads of laundry and
6	worn out washers and dryers
54,000	Dirty diaper changes
19,350	Calls and meetings with Social Workers, Placement workers, Supervisors, Physiotherapists, Family Court Judges and others
12,000	Schedule readjustments
10,000	Times that my children asked, "Can't you get that baby to stop crying?"
10,000	Times where we have said, "How could they have done this to a child?"
5,852	Broken toys
5,250	Times my suits have had baby vomit on them and had to be sent to the cleaners
2,000	Times I went to work or meetings with baby vomit on my suit without my knowledge

3,500	Days and nights on call
3,500	Doctor and clinic appointments
3,500	Sleepless and broken nights
2,500	Kits for Kids
	Training sessions on child development and upgrading
	Chiropractors appointments back problems from lifting babies
4	Broken windows
100,000	Smiles, giggles, hugs, and "I love you's"

Little things can make a big difference

I have discovered that little things can make a big difference. Each day I remind the older children to hold the younger children's hands as they walk across that road. I tell them, "Remember, look both ways." Something simple really, but it has lasting importance.

Sometimes making a difference is as simple as holding someone's hand and crossing the road, or doing so with someone who is going through a hard time. Or sitting with someone who is grieving; or phoning someone who is ill. It really doesn't take much to make a difference. It just takes the willingness to do something. That is all this is about. That is all we have been doing – nothing special. Just little things, that can make a big difference – saying, "I love you," kissing an "owy," or "boo boo," putting on a bandage, changing a diaper – little things – little things that make a big difference.

Lynn came to light up our life at birth. Her parents and half-sister had been living in the city park during the summer and an abandoned building without heat or running water in the winter. They were unable to care for their children. Her parents had no support system of any kind and were developmentally delayed. Her birth mother was very young when she had her first child. The father of Lynn's sister was a convicted pedophile and was still in their life when Lynn was born to her mother by her new boyfriend.

Lynn came to us from the hospital immediately after she was born. Her sister had been placed with another family to be cared for. Her case was more complicated and so it was decided by the courts that they would be separated for the time being. They did, however, have weekly visits with each other.

For almost four years, while her case wound its way through the courts, she was our little girl. During this time her brother was born. He was a full sibling and so whatever was to happen to her would also happen to him. It took nearly four years, but it was finally decided. The two full siblings would be put up for adoption together.

It seems strange – at times, as we raised her, time passed so very slowly. Then later we looked back and wondered where all the time went. Nearly four years had past. We had seen Lynn through her first tooth, her first step, her first word. We saw her through all the diaper changing and the potty training, scraped knees and runny noses. We had hoped and prayed that she would be able to walk and talk. Then, wondered if she would ever sit down and shut up. We took her for her first haircut and dental appointment. We saw her through the crib stage into the big girl bed. Little things really – little things that make a big difference. She was a gift. She was a delight. And now, she was to leave.

The Gift of Love that Broke Our Hearts

It had been an agonizing year. We had thought that we might consider adopting Lynn. However, that was before her brother was born and we knew that they would most probably be adopted together. We had already adopted. We already had five children. We struggled with the question, how could we not adopt her? She had been ours since she was just a few hours old. Yet, we also struggled with our concern about how we could expect her to grow up without knowing her baby brother. It was gut-wrenching. It was literally making Liane sick when she thought of it. We tried to put it out of our minds. Invariably we would find our minds returning to the same questions. We asked ourselves what would be the right and most loving thing to do. We knew that there were couples who couldn't conceive and have children on their own. We knew that she and her baby brother would be loved and cared for as the precious gifts they were. We knew that we would have a voice in who would adopt her. However, how could we give up a child who had come to know us as Mommy and Daddy? And what of our five children that she knew as her sisters and brothers?

We received the call just before Easter that she and her brother were being presented for adoption together. We knew in our hearts it was wrong to separate them. We also knew that we could not adopt two more children at this time. The answer was incontrovertible. She would go with her baby brother to be adopted by another family. It was the right thing to do.

Nearly four years had passed since Lynn had come to us so small and vulnerable. The process leading up to this point had been painfully slow. As my mother would say, "It was as slow as molasses in January." However, once the decision was made the whole thing moved with what seemed like lightning speed. We were in a daze. In what seemed only a few minutes, an adoption conference was called, names were presented, a couple was chosen and the visits began.

The couple who were chosen were both lovely professionals in their early 40s who were unable to have children. They were overwhelmed and grateful. We were ill. The transition into Lynn's adoptive parents' home took longer than it normally would because Lynn had been with us for so long, and because the Children's Aid felt that it was important for Lynn's baby brother to settle in first. Seeing Lynn leave for a few hours was not really all that difficult to cope with. However, as she began the overnight visits everything changed. We reassured ourselves that everything would be OK. And for the most part it was. One overnight became three, and then three became five and then five became a week.

Each time Lynn returned for shorter periods of time as she stayed longer and longer with her adoptive parents. At first, she would come home upset and angry. Later she would just cry. We would call to see how she was doing, not wanting to intrude but doing it anyway. Her new parents were very good to us. They would call to let us know how she was and ask us questions, which we gladly answered, wanting to help them help Lynn adjust.

Once in a while, we would hear Lynn crying and weeping in the background while we were talking to her new parents. She would say, "That Mommy? That Daddy? I go see Mommy, I go see Daddy... please, please!" It was killing us. I began to suffer massive migraines, as did Liane. I would wake up in such pain that I could not open my eyes. No amount of Advil helped. We knew the stabbing pain in our heads was just a symptom of the anguish in our hearts and ache in our arms.

The day came when we were to have our "goodbye visit." Liane went to the clinic for Lynn's medical release and physical. When Lynn saw her she ran and hugged her and cried, "I go home now? I go home now?"

Liane held her in her arms and said, "I love you darling, but no. You must stay with your new mommy and daddy." Lynn slumped down in her chair. Liane then said, "But tonight you will come and see everyone." With that she smiled and brightened somewhat.

Live, Love, Learn, and Leave Behind a Lasting Legacy

Lynn arrived at 4:00 p.m. and would be staying for two hours. She ran in to hug us and kiss us all. She was soon in what had been her bedroom for toys and began playing with our-seven-year-old daughter Tabitha. We chatted with Lynn's parents as we watched her play. Every once in a while she would come up to us and hug us and ask for a kiss. As it approached our normal supper hour, we could see that she was getting hungry. We offered to feed her, but they said no. They told us that they had a long trip out of town and would be eating later. Knowing Lynn as we did, we knew she would never last. We tried to gently encourage them to let her eat. They would have none of it. We backed off. They were her parents now.

The thought of losing Lynn was almost too much for me. I had to leave by 6:00 to be at the church for a wedding rehearsal. It was now 5:30, but I couldn't take it any longer. I went to the bathroom to hide the tears and wash my face. Lynn followed me. "Why Daddy cry?" she asked.

"Daddy sad," I said, as I gathered her into my arms.

She said, "I kiss better." She kissed my eyes and hugged me, putting her little arms around my neck. I held her close.

I thanked her, kissed her and said, "I will *always* love you Darling, but Daddy has to go now, OK?"

She said, "OK, Daddy" and ran and played again with Tabitha.

I couldn't speak. I simply waved to Liane and Lynn's parents as I passed through the front door. Liane knew I had a rehearsal, however, she knew by the expression on my face why I was leaving early. I wept nearly all the way to the church. At one point I had to pull over. I was afraid I would drive into a telephone pole if I didn't. When I arrived at the church the couple was there, happily awaiting my arrival for the rehearsal. No one knew I had just given away my daughter. As their laughter rang through the church and the sun set through the stained glass windows, my heart silently was breaking into little pieces stained in anguish. I later arrived home to a noticeably quieter place. Tabitha sat quietly on the sofa. I asked her if she missed Lynn. She said, "No," but then said to Liane, "Now I have no friends to play with."

We didn't clue in at first. But soon we understood and we said, "You miss playing with Lynn." With that, Tabitha broke down, allowing tears to flood down her face, and ours came as we all grieved together. Liane held her as she cried.

In life it is not what we think or say that counts. It is what we do about what we think or say that counts. It is because our life is made manifest by every action we take. It is what we do that makes a statement about what we truly believe. And it is when we do something to make a difference that we can be assured that something of significance has been left because we existed.

Of course, this doesn't mean that everyone has to win a Nobel Prize for peace or literature, or conceive of some earth-shaking discovery to feel that they have contributed in some manner. It simply means that we do what we are uniquely gifted by God to do. We do not need to be a Curie, King, Mother Teresa, Mandela, or Oprah, or even Dr. Phil in order to make a difference in the world. There are millions of Ms Jones, and Mr. Smiths that will never receive national recognition for what they do; yet they will also leave their indelible mark. Why then do they do it? They do it because they desire to make a difference. It is as simple as that.

Many people have asked, "How can you care for, love and raise a child for years and then allow them to leave? How can you do it? Why do you do it? Doesn't it break your hearts?" The answer is always yes. It does do exactly that. However, it needs to be done. We know we can make a difference. And so we do it even if that means the loss of someone so dear.

I came across a story that describes what I mean very well. It was about Renoir and Matisse, the great French artists. Renoir was a friend of Matisse and one day Renoir went to see Matisse who was suffering from great pain in his hands due to his age, arthritis and illness. Renoir, knowing how much pain Matisse was feeling, and caring for his old friend said, "Why don't you just stop painting? It causes you so much pain."

It is true. Whenever you attempt to create a thing of beauty, whether that is a painting, a family, a mission, or a life, there is pain. But when you focus on the thing of beauty, the pain becomes inconsequential. That is why we know that one day with Lynn, the pain will pass but the beauty will remain. She is a thing of beauty. And she will brighten the life of her parents as she did ours.

God bless you, Lynn. And God bless your mommy and daddy. We love you and them for loving you. And God bless all the Lynns to come who are beings of beauty in this ongoing world of pain.

Everyone needs a place to belong

Life is a journey which starts at home.
~ Charles Handy

We all need a place to belong. It is a strong human need. It reaches to the very depths of our soul. For it contains within it our need for acceptance, affirmation and affection.

In the early 1980s medical researchers at the University of Miami conducted studies on babies who were eight weeks premature. It found that those who were touched, cuddled and held grew 49% more than those who were not. This therapy was called, "kinetic tactile stimulation." It is interesting to note the technical names we use to scientifically replace the word "love."

Jean Vanier said, "Loneliness is a feeling of not being part of anything, of being cut out. It is a feeling of being unworthy, of not being able to cope in the face of a universe that seems to work against us." This need for acceptance, affirmation and affection is a universal need. We all need to know that there is a place on this earth where we belong. This is one of the most important lessons I learned from the children. The need to belong is very powerful. How troubling that it can cause people to accept the unacceptable and endure the intolerable. Noah Ben Shea tells us what belonging ought to mean: "Family is a way of holding hands with forever." Too often, though, it is not.

A Place to Belong

Tracy arrived in our home with her baby brother late one Friday evening from a police raid on a "crack house." She was five years old and her brother two, when they arrived with only the clothes on their backs. She and Jamie were dirty and hungry; they reeked of never having had a bath. Both had lice and scabies, and feces were caked on their little emaciated bodies as if they had swum in a mud puddle and then sat in the sun to bake dry.

Liane met with the social worker to obtain their background and her recommendations for their care. I brought the children something to eat. After the worker left, they were bathed and de-loused using medicated shampoo kept on hand for such situations. As Tracy's hair was being washed, an army of lice began to frantically crawl up my arm. It was disgusting.

Their clothes went outside to the garage and were replaced with new pajamas for each of them to have and wear. They had a difficult time understanding that a teddy bear and toy that they were allowed to pick out was theirs to keep as their very own. We tucked them into bed at three a.m., kissed their foreheads and said a caring good night.

In the morning Tracy sleepily came down the stairs, rubbing her eyes with her little fists, and watched her brother Jamie being fed by Liane. I lowered the newspaper to greet her with "Good morning Tracy." She smiled. Jamie was seated in a highchair being spoon fed. Tracy was transfixed, not used to seeing such loving attention. She was accustomed to waking to see her brother crawling around the apartment for food left in corners or in the garbage, like a dog in an alley, while she lay on her torn mattress that had been thrown against the wall to make it easier for addicts to shoot up.

The sweet aroma of bacon and eggs, normal for us but unusual for her, caused her stomach to growl and her heart to ache. Her first words were filled with sorrow, desperation and dire, open need. They poured out of her as tears fell from her eyes, "Will you be my mommy and daddy? And can we stay here forever? Please!"

Everyone needs to know that "we" belong.

This sudden, desperate plea broke our hearts. As Liane gathered Tracy up into her arms and gave her a loving hug and brought her to the table, we exchanged a troubled look that conveyed what we both knew but wouldn't say. The terrible truth was, she and her brother would not be with us long. And no matter how much our hearts ached for them, and we desired to do more for them, it would not be for us to give them that place to belong. And though it would be the desire of the placement social worker – who is in charge of the placement of children – that Tracy and her brother Jamie be kept together, we couldn't even guarantee that would happen. It would depend on whether there was a home available that could and would take two children. Homes with places for more than one child are quickly filled.

It would be later that day that we would be told what would happen. The good news was that they would be kept together – at least for now. It was clear that for the short term, at least, they would remain in the care of the Children's Aid Society. They would be placed in a foster home and be cared for until the Courts determined what the next step would be. And it would not be until the social workers brought their complete case before the family court judge that their final fate would be determined.

We try to keep track of what happens to the children that come through our home; however, it's not always possible. The lucky ones are adopted or go to live with relatives that have been proven able, after investigation, to provide a safe place for them to be raised. Far too often it takes years to resolve. Sometimes it never occurs. The social workers do their best to gather enough evidence to prove their case, but it is the judge in the family court that makes the final decision. These decisions take too long, and are often wrong – tragically wrong.

The history of child welfare has not been a positive one. It has lurched and stumbled along for years. Though abused children are better off than they were and they do have more legal rights today, it seems that these rights are not consistently enforced or properly applied. This is not surprising, due to the fact that both Canada and the United States had at one time more protection for dogs and cats under the law than children. It was first in the United States and then later in Canada that children became protected under the law as "animals." The first laws protecting children were created under the prevention of cruelty to animals act. Until then, children were considered property. Parents could do whatever they wanted and often did in outrageous ways. What happened to them was less important than what happened to a pet. The law had no means – or desire – to intervene. Legally, things have changed. In reality, however, little has. Judges still do not want to sever the relationship between a parent and child even if the evidence of excessive violence and abuse is present. As a result, the abusive parent is given the de facto right to do whatever they want to a child. Judges do not treat domestic violence against children as a crime. They still let parents who kill their children off *without* jail time. We all remember when violence against women was treated the same way. There was a time when violence against women was at epidemic levels and was not considered a crime but simply a domestic dispute. Thank God the law now has declared it a crime. I pray to God that it will change for children as well. And they will one day have a safe place to belong.

We all need to know that we belong.

No one can survive in life without love. Dr. John Plokker, head of a large mental hospital in Holland said, "The deepest need in human nature is to love and be loved." The need for love is very profound. The need for acceptance, affirmation and affection can cause people to do things they would not otherwise do. And the fear of losing love, or not being connected to it, can also cause people to do things to protect themselves from that loss.

Whenever you enter the lives of those who face difficulties, the possibility of having to deal with things you would rather not stares back at you. We faced this reality when Gabriel arrived in our home at four a.m. He was the perfect little gentleman. He was four years old and spoke perfect English. He reminded me of the child in the movie *Little Lord Fauntleroy*. His patent leather shoes shone below a well-kept cashmere overcoat and knickers. I wondered as I peered at an outfit that cost more than one of my suits, what on earth would cause him to be brought into an emergency home like ours, especially at this hour. The police had been searching for him for some time. They were not able to tell us more at the time.

We did as we always did at that hour when a child came into our care. We offered him food and got him ready for bed. As we were reaching to change his diaper he began to scream in terror, yelling, "No! No!" We decided not to change him then, given that there was no obvious smell or need to change the diaper. He soon settled, but when we placed him in bed he began to cry out for his father. I comforted him, as did my wife Liane, until he eventually settled and slept. In the morning we were informed that the father was under investigation because there appeared to be evidence that Gabriel had been bred for sex with a pedophile. The news reported that a child had been apprehended by the police and Children's Aid. The father was being charged with abuse. They reported that he had paid a woman to have a child so he could adopt him. Later there seemed to be enough evidence to cause the authorities to fear that, without the knowledge of the woman who had been asked to be a surrogate parent, the father had made plans to raise and use this child for the purpose of sex.

Yet, each night Gabriel called out for his "father."

Gabriel left us and was later placed in the care of his grand-parents. We were however horrified to discover that his "father" a few weeks later was released from jail and sentenced by the courts to remain with them as well until trial. We never did find out if that meant Gabriel had to be moved.

We have discovered to our shock and utter amazement that children can be horribly abused, mistreated, and harmed and still that aching longing to belong remains.

We need to tread softly when we deal with one another. We never know what the other person has gone through. W.B. Yeats put it this way;

> *Had I the heaven's embroidered cloths*
> *Enwrought with golden and silver light,*
> *The blue and the dim and the dark cloths*
> *Of night and light and half light,*
> *I would spread the cloths beneath your feet:*
> *But I, being poor, have only my dreams;*
> *I spread my dreams under you feet;*
> *Tread softly because you tread on my dreams*

People will do almost anything and fearfully put up with the worst of things just because their need for love is so profound. Is it any wonder many search for love in the wrong places and for the wrong reasons? Perhaps if we knew that there was one place that we belonged, where we were loved and comforted, it would make all the difference.

If a child has never had a place to belong and is moved from one home to another, they will eventually reject any sign of affection because they fear that if they let it in and trust the people offering it they will only be hurt again. It is no surprise then, that we have so many angry children and violent young adults acting out their frustrations at school, home or rampaging on the street today.

People search for love as if it were a city lost beneath the desert dunes. Each child rediscovers it, each person recovers it, each couple redefines it, each parent reinvents it. The word can mean nothing, or it can mean everything. We say it in relation to things we eat and wear, and to those we eat with. We say, "I love Baskin and Robbins ice cream. I love that sweater. I'd love to go skiing." Or "Daddy loves you." It can be such a sloppy word. Yet, it can be so wonderful.

"How much do you love me?" a child asks. And we say as we fling open our arms in glee and stretch out our fingers to their furthest point to try to grasp the world and bring it in, "I love you this much!"

Or, we say, "Think of the biggest thing you can think of and then double, no, triple, no, a hundred times that is how much I love you!"

When Elizabeth Barrett Browning wrote her famed sonnet, "How do I love thee?" she didn't "count the ways" because she had a mind for math. It was because as an English poet she was trying to convey in her words and to search for ways to tell of her love for her beloved.

Dr. Albert Schweitzer said, "We are all so much together, but we are all dying of loneliness." That is why love is so powerful. We all seek to have it. We all need it. Love is perhaps the basic human need because, "Life minus love is zero."

The great psychiatrist, Karl Menninger, declared that "Love cures people – both the ones who give it and the ones who receive it." Are you familiar with the quote by the Roman statesman and philosopher, Lucius Annaeus Seneca? "It is better to have loved and lost than never to have loved at all." It is better because at least we can live on with the remembrance of having been loved.

Throughout history people have written about, sung about, and thought about love more than perhaps any other single human need and emotion. Where would the music industry be without the airwaves filled with love or lack of it?

A professor of sociology while teaching a class on community and life asked his students, "What is love?"

One student said, "Love is dancing cheek to cheek amidst stardust."

Another said, "Life is one thing after another, love is two things after each other."

And a third student replied, "Love is a feeling you feel, when you feel you're going to feel, a feeling you have never felt before."

Is it any wonder we are confused about life and love, and where we belong? It is because, when the diapers have to be changed, and the garbage has to be taken out and the work has to be done, the feeling you felt when you felt you were going to feel a feeling you never felt before vanishes. And then you wonder if love is only a feeling. It is not. It is a choice we make and a firm commitment we take.

Tracy, Jamie and Gabriel reminded us of this commitment. We had made a commitment to her and her brother and Gabriel the moment they walked through our door, and to all the others who would come through our door, that this would be a place where love lived. This would be a place where they would belong, even if that meant for just a few days. They would know, even if they would not experience it again for years, that there was someone who loved them, and if they could hold on to it, remember it, and cherish it in their heart, they would find it again.

The Power Behind the Work

The world can be a very unfriendly and lonely place. And knowing that you are not alone in the universe can make a big difference. I discovered that having a sense of belonging can truly make a difference. And for me that began when I came to understand that I belonged to God, and that God was watching out for me.

When the great philosopher and theologian Augustine was a boy, he and his mother were preparing for a long journey from home. Augustine expressed fear his mother would die far from home. His mother said, "Son, no one is ever far from God. So I will never die far from home."

Wordsworth had this to say,

> *Our birth is but a sleep and a forgetting*
> *The soul rises with us hath elsewhere its setting*
> *And cometh from afar*
> *Not in entire forgetfulness*
> *Not in utter nakedness*
> *but trailing clouds of glory do we come*
> *From God Who is our home.*

God is our home. Here on earth and in heaven. For as St. Paul said, "... it is in Him that we live and move and have our being." Once we have grasped that we belong; we have a renewed power to do the work that each of us is gifted and called to do.

The Purpose of the Work: Belonging

Some ponder how we could possibly have cared for nearly 1,000 children. "How do you endure the loss of the children that you have helped to become whole again only to watch them be returned to the abuse that they came from? How can you not want to just cry out at that type of injustice? And yet, you are still willing at midnight to receive another child and do it all over again. How can you raise a child and watch them leave you to be held in the arms of an adoptive mother and endure the ache in your own? How can you bear the sight of another child with a broken arm and a cracked skull?"

Our response becomes, "How can we not? Was it not Mother Teresa who said, 'What we do is nothing but a drop in the ocean, but if we didn't do it, the ocean would be one drop less.' When we look into the face of a child, see her smile, hear her giggle and have her reach out for our hand, how can we not do everything we can."

Everyone needs acceptance

All babies are the same. All adults aren't. When an infant arrives in our arms wrapped in a hospital blanket early in the morning, her parents may be Catholic, Protestant, Muslim, Buddhist, Jewish, Black, white, Asian, bi-racial, rich or poor. She is, however, to us just a baby in need of our care. She doesn't comprehend any difference between us. So that begs the question, "Is there?"

The history of humanity may indeed be said to be one of exclusion not inclusion, rejection rather then reception, hate rather then love, aggression instead of compassion. Throughout history every society has created a civilization of exclusion. Within every group in any society there is a list of those that are to be excluded. And you are only kidding yourself if you think that you are not on one of those lists. We are all on someone's list. That list may be based on race or religion. It may include the Muslim, the Jew, the Palestinian, or the Christian. It may include the less privileged among us or the poor, or immigrant. It may include the young, or old, the disabled, those with AIDS, the over-weight, the homosexual. The lists can be endless and the hunger for acceptance can be agonizing.

There is a moving story in Luke's Gospel that Jesus tells. There was a beggar by the name of Lazarus. He was poor, des-titute and hungry. His legs were covered with sores. Across the road was a very wealthy man who used to have large gatherings.

Lazarus would have liked to have had just a little of what the rich man had. Yet, he was never offered any. Lazarus died and went to be in the "heart of Abraham," where he experienced perfect peace. Not long after the rich man also died. He went to "the place of torment." When the rich man looked up, he saw Lazarus in perfect peace and called out, "Father Abraham please send Lazarus down to put some water on my lips for I am in pain!" Abraham responded, "It is impossible. Between you and him there is an abyss that nobody can cross." Abraham could have gone on to say, that this abyss was also present while you were alive.

Today, there remains an abyss between us all in one way or another. This abyss remains between rich and poor, those who have and those who have not, between white and black and Asian, race and religion. It is an abyss, however, that can be crossed – though not easily.

It can only be crossed by those who have found that place of acceptance within themselves; who have that strength of spirit that affords them the ability to offer that acceptance to someone else. We, who have that sense and place of acceptance, are the only ones who can offer it to those who don't have it. We, who have what we need, are the only ones who can help the others learn how to get what they need. It is like one beggar telling another beggar where to find food; for after all is said and done, we are all the same. We are all broken, hurting human beings looking for the same thing. I learned this from caring for children.

Aung San Suu Kyi, the Buddhist who won the Nobel Peace Prize for her struggle for peace, human rights and democracy in Burma says, "All barriers of race and religion can be overcome when people work together in common endeavours, based on love and compassion. Together we can help to develop a happier, better world, where greed and ill-will and selfishness are minimized. This is not impractical idealism; it is a down-to-earth recognition of our greatest needs.

Some times it takes courage to grapple with the difficulties that lie in the path of development. Unpopular decisions may have to be made and prejudices overcome. It may be necessary to defy despotic governments, to stand by the downtrodden and the under-privileged in the face of oppression and injustice. But "perfect love casts out fear, and everything becomes possible when charitable projects are carried out with true charity in the heart."[1]

"Perfect love casts out fear." Fear is the problem. Love is the solution.

The Fear That Imprisons Us

I have discovered that we are most afraid of the unfamiliar. The trouble begins when we allow that fear to imprison us and then give birth to prejudice.

Due to our work with infants, we have come in contact with some of the advantaged and disadvantaged within every race, culture and religion in Canada. We have cared for children from every walk of life.

What I have learned is that none of this matters. We all come into this world with a need for love, security and acceptance, and food, shelter, and clothing. Everything else is learned.

We grow up with such a narrow view of the world. We very often grow up within our own culture, race, religion and country. Everything seems safe and familiar. Anything outside that sphere is unfamiliar and frightening. We build walls to keep us from being influenced by other cultures. We do this because we somehow fear that if we don't, we will be contaminated. These walls thicken and eventually harden into a granite-like prejudice.

We were never born with this fear of the unfamiliar. Children are naturally fearless. They start out in an unfamiliar world having to learn how to do everything. Everything is new to them. Everything is a new discovery.

Children are born with only two fears; the fear of falling and the fear of loud noises. All other fears are learned. We learn fear of other people and prejudice toward other cultures at an early age. And it is often because of the fear of the unfamiliar.

Rejection of Others and Acceptance of Self

When someone experiences rejection by another person or group, one of two things happens. Either they accept the view of the person doing the rejecting and then internalize the rejection. Or they reject the rejection.

Too often people internalize the rejection. This leads to a sense of inferiority and lack of self-respect. Eventually, this inferiority will give way to despair, depression and/or anger. This anger, left unchecked, might eventually result in a destructive or self-destructive action. This is the case for many of the older children we see. After years of rejections, first by their parents then by others, the result is an angry child who strikes out at the world around them.

However, a person with a strong sense of self will reject the rejection. They will state in effect, "Your rejection of me has more to say about you than it does about me." This allows for the person being rejected to retain their self-respect.

In *Becoming Human,* Jean Vanier writes, "Some of the oppressed, instead of acknowledging their hatred of the oppressor and their desire for revenge, get stuck in feelings of inferiority. Oppression has penetrated their own hearts. Convinced that they are inferior, they remain unable to react or to struggle for their rights."[2]

Once a person accepts the inaccurate view that they are inferior, because of the abuse they have experienced or their culture, race, religion or sexual orientation, they internalize that inferiority and become angry at themselves and the world.

The stark reality of this came home to us when we had to deal with this first hand. We sent our three youngest children to vacation summer bible school one summer at another church. Our youngest, Tabitha, was four at the time. At the end of the day when they were getting ready for me to pick them up, my oldest son Nathanael, eight, was confronted by another boy. The boy said angrily, "Who is that little girl to you?"

Noticing the anger in his voice, Nathanael sheltered Tabitha behind his back and said, "She's my sister."

The boy yelled, "She can't be! She's black and you're white!"

To which Tabitha stuck her head out from behind her big brother and said, "I'm not black, I'm caramel, and you're not white, you're peach. I know my colours; I'm in junior kindergarten now!"

Nathanael hushed her, "We have got to go."

The boy continued by grabbing him by the shoulder. "She's not your sister. She's black," and then punched him in the face. Aaron, who was seven, ran to his brother and sister, and together they left for the street just as I arrived. I noticed Nathanael holding his face, and asked him what happened.

"Nothing," he replied. Then later he told us the whole story as we arrived home. I was furious. I told him how proud I was of him and his brother for protecting Tabitha and hugged Tabitha as I told her how proud I was of her for standing up for herself and correcting the meanness of the boy. I also hugged both my boys.

Given that it was the last day of vacation bible school and the children did not know the last name of the boy, I could do little but inform the church about what had happened. I don't know whether I was more angry at the violence, or the racism that still remains in the church.

We are all human beings, created by God. Have we not learned that when we hate another because of race, creed or colour, we are really hating ourselves? The lesson here is that children learn, through what they live.

I had long since thought that racism was out of our churches in Canada, until I was approached to consider moving to a very prestigious church from another part of the country to be their senior minister. A few of the search committee arrived at my present church and remained for the coffee hour. While speaking to one of the representatives during the coffee hour, Tabitha approached and asked, "Daddy, give me a hug?" I reached down, picked her up and gave her a big hug.

I looked up to see the look of horror on the face of the member of the search committee who asked, "Who is she?"

"She's my daughter," I said, "isn't she beautiful?"

To which he replied curtly, "Thank-you, Dr. Niles." He gathered his other committee member and left in a hurry, not looking back. I received a rejection letter the next day by express post.

I wasn't shocked by receiving the letter. I was shocked only by the speed of its arrival. Though I was angry and disappointed at their racism, I was relieved that I had found it out before accepting the position. How could I accept a post in a place that would ostracize my daughter because of her skin colour? Nor would I want Tabitha or my other children to have to be in a place that openly teaches those life values through their behaviour, words or actions.

Tabitha came to us at birth. She was a beautiful bi-racial Jamaican-Canadian. We immediately fell in love with her. We tell her that God grew her in our hearts, just like God grew her sisters in Mommy's tummy. We would also tell her that love has all the colours of the rainbow.

It had taken nearly four years before the courts finally made a decision about who would become her parents. We had long since made ours, deciding that she would always have a place to belong. If she was to return to her birth-mother, which we knew was highly unlikely, and later return to the Children's Aid Society, we would be the ones to receive her. We had decided that if she was to be raised in care, it would be by us. And if, as we had hoped, she was to be adopted, it was going to be by Liane and me. She was always going to have a place to belong. We have encouraged her to accept herself as God created her, in spite of what others may think of her. And to our delight and relief, she has.

The courts made the decision that she was to be adopted. The wheels were then set in motion for us to adopt her.

We were the lucky ones. We know far too well how difficult it is for a child, once caught in the web-like net of the court system, to break free. Hundreds of children fall through the cracks of our legal system and get entangled in the net of the legal bureaucracy hanging below. The legal system fails to realize how injurious and detrimental the delays are on these children. The legal system perpetuates and participates in the abuse when it allows it to continue due to its unwillingness to make a decision. A judge has the responsibility to make a decision in the best interest of the child. Children who are left in limbo for years due to indecision are forever damaged. They are damaged not only by losing the opportunity of having a stable family and home through adoption, but they are damaged by the constant movement from biological home to foster home, back to biological home, and then a different foster home.

Severing the parental rights is a very serious decision to make. Only a judge can make the decision. When they fail or refuse to make that decision because of dangerously outmoded beliefs that date back to the Middle Ages, when children, like women, were considered property, we have a recipe for disaster.

With Tabitha, the disaster was averted. She would not have to experience the ongoing disruption of moving from home to home. She would not become damaged by internalizing this type of rejection, like so many others, because of their racial heritage – which so often happens to bi-racial children like Tabitha – or history of abuse. There would not be that sense of inferiority and lack of self-respect which gives way to despair, depression and/or anger. This same anger, when left unchecked, might eventually result in a destructive or self-destructive action.

The reason for this is clear. Tabitha has learned since birth that she is accepted and loved just as she is.

The American writer Patricia Raydon in her book, *My First White Friend: Confessions on Race, Love and Forgiveness,* wrote how she had learned to hate white people due to the cruel subjugation of living in a part of the United States with a long history of racism. She writes, "I hated them because they lynched and lied and jailed and poisoned and neglected and discarded and excluded and exploited countless cultures and communities with such blatant intent or indifference as to humanly defy belief or understanding."[3]

She, however, began to realize that this hatred was tearing her apart inside. It was damaging her identity and self-respect. It was also getting in the way of gestures of friendship that a white girl in high school was offering. She stated that she needed to stop waiting for the white people to ask for forgiveness, and instead ask for forgiveness for her own hatred and her inability to see a white person as just that, a person.

We have a choice. We can choose to be imprisoned by our anger, or we can choose to accept ourselves.

1   Aung San Suu Kyi, Nobel Peace Prize acceptance speech
2   Vanier, Jean, *Becoming Human,* (Anansi Press Limited, 1998) p.143
3   Raybon, Patricia, *First White Friend: Confessions on Race, Love and Forgiveness,* (New York Viking Press, 1996)

LESSON FOUR

Build a life not a résumé

You make a living by what you get,
you make a life by what you give.
~ Winston Churchill

Most of us can look back to our childhood experiences and remember at least one moment when a person or event changed the course of our lives. It may have been a word of encouragement, an offer of assistance, or an expression of affection. And at that moment everything changed. For it was at that moment that you began to believe that you were a valued, esteemed and treasured human being. For some people, however, that moment never comes. For some, it is the one thing missing.

Jordan was a thirty-five-day-old baby. He weighed just four pounds two ounces when he died. He was four ounces less at his death than he was when he was born. He was born in one of the wealthiest cities in Canada. Yet, Jordan starved to death. It seems impossible that it could have happened here. His mother, a teenager, had been living on the streets for three years before giving birth. She was a child having a child. She had no support and no family. She had no one to teach her how to feed, protect and care for her child. Her poverty and desperation caused her – we are told – to water down the formula she fed him. The result – her baby died.

Why did this happen? Why didn't anyone do something? Why didn't someone see what was going on? Why didn't someone say something? We live in a wonderful country. Yet the care, protection and welfare of children remains a great concern. It is of great concern for me. And if you are a parent, I know it is to you as well. And even it you are not, I know you care.

I often think of Jordan whenever a police officer or social worker arrives at my home at 3 a.m. with a child wrapped in a hospital blanket. When I look at the innocent little child in my arms, I think of what has been missing in his or her life. I think of what this child and every one of us needs to develop into a fully actualized human being.

Too much of life is spent on what is trivial instead of what is truly important. We expend vast amounts of energy working on ways to gain a measure of acceptance by peers and other professionals. We strive to acquire degrees that declare our intelligence, and titles that express our importance. We seek positions of power to give us the illusion of security. And we do it all at the expense of a life that's worthy. What is important to you? What is it that you are really after? Everyone wants and needs affection, affirmation and attention. We may seek to find these things in different ways, but we continue seeking them out.

A child taught me this lesson. Tani came to us late one night from the world-renowned "Sick Kids Hospital." The social worker that accompanied her was in tears as she told us of some of her injuries. Tani was six months old, yet she looked only half that age, tiny, thin and emaciated. Her arm was in a cast. We were told that she would have to be returned the next day for a full skeletal scan. The social worker believed she had more broken bones. We were confused that she never a made sound throughout the night. Was she not suffering? None of us imagined the amount of pain she had been in. She whimpered as they took the x-rays. Why had she not learned how to cry? The nurses wept and the doctor's eyes teared as they had to bend her arms and legs to allow for a full picture. We were horrified at what was revealed. Nearly every bone in her body had been broken at one point in her young life; some were fresh others, not.

Over the course of the next six months we watched as she emerged from her shell. It was more than a week later before she allowed herself to cry out. It took only a few more cries for her to trust that she would not be hurt again. All she needed was a safe place to grow and develop and to be held, loved, and cared for. But isn't that true for all of us?

A safe place is necessary for us to grow and develop into the person we are meant to be. We all need to be loved, held and cared for as we seek to become all that we can be. Too often we look for these things in the wrong places and, sadly, in the wrong way. Instead of building a life, we focus on building a résumé of status, place and envy. We think that if we have the right education, profession and possessions that we will be given the attention, affection, and affirmation that we long for. The problem is we are wrong.

Over the course of the last fifteen years I have had the sacred privilege of being at the side of hundreds of beds before people crossed over. And I can tell you from experience that I have never met a person who said belatedly, "I wish I had gone to more meetings. I wish I had made more business contacts. I wish I got that prominent position that I was wanting. I wish I had worked more."

On the contrary, I have found them saying, "I wish I had lived differently. I wish I had spent more time with my family. I wish I had been more involved in my children's lives. I wish I had lived my dream instead of giving up on it. I wish I had risked more. I wish I had made more of a difference. I wish I had spent time thinking about spiritual things, so that I would not be so afraid of the prospect of death, and question the legacy I leave behind."

They wished that they had found out early what was truly

important in life. As some of them looked back they discovered their time was spent building a résumé for the next job, instead of improving the relationship with the people who were most important to them. Rather then spending their time on those things that are meant to sustain them in life and remain after death, faith, family and friends and making a difference, they had overlooked or taken for granted what so clearly stood before them.

We too often fail to do the things that can be most fulfilling to us. For some reason we don't believe we either have the right to do so, or the ability to do it. Let me let you in on a secret. You have the right to live a life that is full and fulfilling – and you have the ability to achieve it. Your life is God's gift to you. What you do with it is your gift to God.

I learned this lesson from Brian.

I was still struggling with my own clarity of purpose when we were approached by a social worker to accept caring for Brian. I had finally given up the need to build a résumé, but had not yet truly come to comprehend the importance of building a life. Though I thought I was doing so, it seemed that for some time I had been sleepwalking through life doing what was right in front of me but not gaining a sense of the measure of its importance.

Brian was born premature due to his mother's chronic drug and alcohol use. He was born with some bleeding on the brain, and also diagnosed with cerebral palsy. We were told that he would likely be developmentally delayed. He arrived in our home at nine months old and remained with us until his case was settled in the courts and he was available for adoption.

Children's Aid had asked us to care for him due to the fact that he was medically fragile. We were told that he would have many medical appointments. A physiotherapist would work with him twice a week in our home. We would have to learn the phys-iotherapy techniques so that we could provide therapy between his visits and appointments. It would mean enduring his screams and tears as he struggled against the pain inflicted by the physiotherapist for his own good. Awaking in the night he whimpered and cried out for us to hold him as he ached from the treatment. It would mean having to walk around, at times exhausted, because we heeded his cries to hold and rock him until the pain passed and he rested fitfully in our arms.

Such gruelling work meant organizing our lives around the needs of this child. It would mean scheduling not only the medical and therapy appointments, but visits from social workers. It would mean having more than the usual branch meetings at Children's Aid with workers, supervisors and lawyers as they prepared to develop the case for the court to sever the ties with Brian's mother that would allow him to be adopted. It meant setting up weekly visits with the mother at the centre so she could see him. It meant getting him ready and driving him to the visits even if she didn't show up or was too drunk or high to see him when she did. It meant affidavits for court and a possible court appearance if we were witness to anything she said or did during these visits that was important for determining his future welfare, which had happened in the past with other children.

We also had our own children to think of. It would mean that the time Liane and I had for each other and for ourselves would, while we cared for Brian, be spent on our own children. We did not want them to lose out because of what we had decided to do.

For twelve months our life was a scheduling nightmare. Even though we had agreed to care for Brian we were begged not to give up doing the emergency night duty. It is nearly impossible for Children's Aid to find homes to do emergency night duty as backup when we are full. The thought of our not doing it for a year may well have driven the night duty placement supervisor – who in our minds is a saint – to have a coronary.

Each evening we would be on call as the primary emergency home for our city of three million people for infants up to five-year-olds. When Children's Aid closed their doors, we opened. We remained on call twenty-four hours a day on weekends, and throughout the night on weekdays. If we received a child at night or at three in the morning, we would care for that child until the workers or courts had a permanent placement for them.

This was always in the back of our mind. Most of the time we rarely gave it a second thought. If it happened, we'd deal with it. However, when we were exhausted, it could gnaw at us like a bleeding ulcer. Each night after we had finished doing Brian's physiotherapy, fed him, changed him and put him to bed, we focused our attention on the other children. We were committed to spending time with them, helping our own children and the other children with homework, playing with them, or simply enjoying time together as well as dealing with the occasional outburst of teenage angst.

Once that was done and the five younger children were all put to bed and our older teenagers were working on their homework, we would then turn our attention on the next day's schedule. We could never work on a weekly schedule, our life was too involved for that. With at least seven children to think of at any given time, as well as the multitude of other events and appointments, scheduling became an art. We work on a daily and often an hourly schedule. At times it seemed as if we were "tag-team" parenting. Either Liane or I would drive the children to school in the morning while the other one remained home with the babies. If we received a child at some point the night before, Liane or I would take the child that arrived at night to the clinic for a physical after dropping off the children at school. She or I would field phone calls from workers and supervisors, sometimes referring them to Liane if she was at or en route to the clinic. At the same time I would be rescheduling my appointments to an hour or two later, or the next day, adjusting this as needed and doing my paperwork at home rather than at the office. All the while bathing, feeding and changing diapers.

After Liane returned home, I would leave for my office and attend to the appointments that I had for that part of the day. After which, I would return home to see Liane waiting to hand me an infant as she left to make her next appointment. Later that afternoon, she would return home only for me to leave to go to my next appointment and pick the children up from school. In between we would again change diapers, bath, dress, feed, field phone calls and do paperwork.

Often our evenings were free to spend with the children; however, there were evenings that one or the other of us would leave for a meeting or training sessions, always one staying at home.

Before falling spent and exhausted into bed we would pull out our list of appointments and meetings for the next day. Liane and I would discuss what appointment I had that could be changed if we received a child that evening, and which of the appointments I had to keep. She told me which appointments with doctors, workers, and physiotherapists were happening that needed me and when I must be home to care for the other children while she met with workers or doctors.

To a lesser degree this had been our life for many years. However, Brian's fragile medical condition seemed to put everything in hyper-drive. It caused us to let things of lesser importance fall away, and motivated us to focus on those things that were truly essential.

Brian was called a "failure to thrive" baby. That meant that no matter what anyone had tried to do for him in the past nothing seemed to work. He was not getting better, stronger or healthier. It was for that reason that he came to us. He arrived kicking and screaming. He looked petite and impish. He was all legs and arms, a jumbled mass of uncoordinated body parts seemingly flailing at the injustice of his start in life. We loved him the moment we saw him. Well, most of us. One of our children after one look said, "Yuk! What's his problem?"

The year past quickly and Brian grew and developed significantly. It didn't take long for us all to fall deeply in love with him.

All the devotion, compassion and care, doctors and therapist appointments had done their job. He was developing at a normal rate and the concern over the severity of his Cerebral Palsy had lessened. He would be slower than some children physically and mentally but he offered love like no other. He would giggle and laugh and his impish smile would light up the room when he raced half crawling and half swimming to greet you to get a hug.

The uneasy day arrived when we were to meet with workers to help decide who would be his new parents. We were presented with one wonderful couple. Due to his limitations we had been worried that no one would want to adopt Brian. We knew this was a very real possibility. We had even thought of adopting him ourselves. Yet, we had adopted already and now had five children of our own and would often say that we have been so blessed that we wanted others to experience this blessing as well.

We knew that it would be difficult to find someone to adopt him because of his limiting physical and mental conditions. The sad reality is that many people want to adopt newborn white girls. Children who were "damaged" or were mixed in race or over the age of four years old rarely were adopted. Imagine being "over the hill" or too old at age four! It happens far too often and these children risk getting lost in a system that is not prepared, nor equipped, to raise children from infancy to adulthood.

There are not enough loving homes in our society that are willing to welcome these children into their lives and provide a place of safety for them. Some of the lucky children, who have not been bounced in and out of the care of Children's Aid, have stayed with one family during those four years. They are often adopted by that family. The rest, tragically, can be, and often are, bounced around like an unwanted beach ball on a turbulent lake because the courts are unable or unwilling to make a rational decision.

That is not, of course, the desire of those in the leadership of the "Society," however, it is unfortunately the reality. It is a reality that needs a great deal of change, not in ten years but starting now.

That was not going to be the case for Brian. We had decided that we were going to do whatever was necessary for him, no matter how long it took. We prayed and hoped that there would be a wonderful couple ready to give him all the love that he himself deserved and wanted to give. Our prayers were answered and an amazing couple came forward. They were perfect. They had adopted once before and wanted a brother for their son. They understood completely the challenges ahead of them, and after they agreed to adopt Brian we helped them set up support systems with Children's Aid so that if the challenges got too great in the future, they could access support from the therapists and doctors without difficulty.

Initially, they began the period of transition toward adoption by coming to our home and visiting for an hour or two with Brian. Later they took him out for an ice cream or to spend time playing at the park, happy that their first experience went well. A week later they had him for a sleepover and returned him the next day. This went on until he spent greater and greater lengths of time with his parents and fewer days and hours with us. Each time he left the safety of our home we would pack more of his toys and clothes to go with him so that his new bedroom would soon look more like his old one.

Happy Wife Happy Life

As I watched Liane prepare to say goodbye to another baby that we had so lovingly cared for, I found myself again thinking how remarkable she was and how happy our life had been. After nearly 20 years of marriage I have learned that if you have a happy wife, you will have a happy life. If she is not happy, then nobody is happy.

Liane continually amazes me. To me she is clearly the best mother on earth. That is why I don't understand why Oprah never picked her to be honoured on one of her mother's day specials. I did, after all, send close to 50 emails one year to convince Oprah about how wondrous Liane truly is. I can only think that those who had to read the millions of emails that people send each year to her thought that I was exaggerating when I said that she was the mother of nearly 1000 children. Who could possibly believe that could be the truth?

Amazing in so many ways, she selflessly cares for not only me and our five children but all the other abused and disadvantaged babies that come our way. She does this with complete devotion, Herculean energy, comprehensive care and unconditional love. She never wavers. When the crying of the fetal alcohol babies becomes like 50 sets of fingernails on a chalkboard, she simply picks them up and rocks them until they are soothed and blissfully drift off to sleep. When the baby becomes sick in the middle of the night, she gets up without complaint and gets medicine. She rarely, if ever, puts herself first.

Her greatest joy is finding a sale at Baby Gap or Oshkosh or some Fisher Price toy or some children's stores so she can buy ten sets of various sized clothes for the children who come into our care. She loves to dress the babies in what we believe every baby deserves – the best. These clothes then stay with the child when they leave. She loves when the doctors and nurses comment on how beautiful the children are in the clothes she buys; and comes away broken-hearted if they make no comment at all. She has often said, "Every child is beautiful, however, some do need a little help to get there. And that is where Baby Gap comes in." She is astounding. My job of finding the money for these things can, at times, be a bit daunting.

The tearful goodbye arrived sooner then we could have planned for Brian. We bathed him, and dressed him in his brand new baby clothes bought especially for him during one of Liane's famous buying trips. We held, kissed, hugged, and finally watched as he waved his little hand and shined his impish smile at us as the car slowly drove away.

Our heart was full while our home seemed somewhat emptier. Liane and I had a few extra hours as a result of only having one child at home and the others in school; so we went shopping for baby cloths. While doing so, Liane found this poem by an anonymous writer that seemed to sum up the change that Brian had brought to our life.

A Heart for Children

One hundred years from now
It will not matter
What kind of car I drove,
How much I had in my bank
Nor what my clothes looked like.
One hundred years from now
It will not matter
What kind of school I attended,
What kind of typewriter I used,
How large or small my church,
But the world may be
A little better because
I was important in the life of a child.

Upon returning home Liane held out this plaque and said, "This is for you," as she give me a kiss. I was overwhelmed. The words said it all. It really is so much better to build a life instead of a résumé. Then the phone rang.

Play every day

Why do children like to play? Each morning, even before they are fully awake, my children will appear from upstairs and ask, "Daddy, can we go out and play?" They don't necessarily know what they want to play or who they are going to play with; they just want to play. They approach the day as an adventure.

It is only later when life closes in on them that they are slower to arise in the morning. It is then, when they begin to be bogged down with problems, school, homework, and chores, that the smile falls from their face, their spirits sags and the enthusiasm for life evaporates. Play is important. A lesson I learned from the children we care for.

Many come to us never having had a toy to play with or time to enjoy it. Imagine being five years old and being the primary caregiver for your baby brother. It happens more often than you think. I am reminded of a little girl named Sally who sat quietly cooing and comforting her baby bother as we spoke to her social worker. We initially took no notice of how adept she was at caring for him. It was only when he started to cry and she placed him in his car seat and looked searchingly around the room. She spotted the refrigerator and headed for it with bottle in hand. We watch in awe as she opened the door of the refrigerator took out the milk and poured it into the bottle, and put the milk back. It was only when we broke from our stunned collective daze that Liane took the bottle and sat her down. Handing her a toy she said, "Darling, it's okay. We'll take care of you and your little brother. You don't have to watch over him while we're here. You can play and have some fun." She stared blankly as if she had never heard that word "play" before, nor been given the permission to enjoy it.

The mother was an addict and prostitute and would often leave the children to fend for themselves, either because she was passed out in a drug-induced stupor or because she was "making" the money to have a "score."

Liane gathered the baby in her arms and began to feed him as I took his sister by the hand and brought her to our toy room. I introduced her to Tabitha and the others and asked if she would like to stay and play with some of the toys or watch a Disney movie. At first she just stared with her mouth open and her eyes wide. I'm sure it must have seemed as if she had just walked into Toyland or Santa's workshop.

"You mean, I can play with any of these?"

"Yes. You can play with any toy you want. Or you can watch any of the children's movies."

I walked with her to the movie shelf that has grown to be quite full as our children have grown older. She chose a movie and I put it on. And we went over to the toys and picked a few for her to play with. A smile crossed her face, as she hesitantly began to play. Her bother cried and she started to get up. I said, "It's okay, darling. Liane's there. He'll be alright." The concern began to leave her face as she returned to playing.

Part of what we do in our care of children is to help the child become a child again. We help them rediscover the importance of playing. I have found that it is not a child's broken bones due to abuse that is their greatest problem, but their shattered spirit that is the most debilitating dilemma to deal with.

Children know intuitively and instinctively that play is important. So, why do we, as adults, give up on it so easily? The "work" of every child is to play happily. However, as adults we work in order to earn the right to play. And some of us work so long and determinedly we leave no time to play. What would happen if we decided to become like a child again and change our work hours into playtime? For some it would mean making major changes. For others it might simply be a change of attitude. Remember the word "attitude." This entire book was written to show how the development of your attitude is yours to discover – and to use properly.

To make your work your play is to approach the day with the exuberance, enjoyment and enthusiasm of most children. It means that we need to see life as a constant source of separate adventures. It means getting rid of the things that are in the way of our playing, and focusing on what is used to enhance it.

If you look at the people who are truly enjoying life, you will discover, as I have, that they are the ones that are doing what they love. They are doing what they truly enjoy doing. An inner smile surrounds their hearts.

LESSON SIX

Pray every day

On hearing that we have cared for so many children, people say, "You must have great patience."

To which I reply, "No, just great prayers. The greatest of which is HELP."

God and I have an ongoing argument that arises when a child comes to our home at three in the morning. She could have a cast on her leg and arm. Cigarette burns may cover fifty percent of her body and she's spent her life in constant hunger.

I say, "God, what were you thinking? What were you thinking, creating someone who would do this to a child? Couldn't you have just stopped them from being born?"

And I'd let God reply, "Yes, but then this child wouldn't be able to be born and come into your arms to be loved and to give love. She wouldn't then go on to be adopted into a loving home to parents who couldn't have children."

"Well, couldn't you have just given the child to them in the first place?"

"Yes, but then the original parents wouldn't have been given the opportunity not to be as awful as they were."

"Well, couldn't you have stopped them from doing it?'

"No, because it is all about free will." This argument normally continues until after Liane or I put the child to bed and I fall asleep. I never win. However, I still can't always prevent my anger from taking control of my outrage.

I don't know if I could do this work if it wasn't for prayer. I have always viewed prayer as universal, essential and something very personal. It provides a bridge to the Eternal. It provides me with a means of receiving the needed resources, guidance and direction from my Lord and Saviour. It has nurtured some of my grandest visions and provided meaning and purpose to the various activities that I do everyday.

Prayer, like a diamond, has many facets. Its beauty is found in its diversity and cut. Prayer can be petition, intercession, thanksgiving, and adoration. It can be a conversation, an argument, a debate. It can simply be a place to wait. It can be a place of rest, restoration and meditation. It is a way of connecting to something that is higher, wiser, and more powerful then any one solitary human being.

Prayer answers the questions, "Is anybody there? Does anybody care?" by coming back with a resounding, "Yes!"

I was asked once with some sarcasm and judgment attached, "Why doesn't God do something to combat the abuse of children?"

To which I said, "He did. He created *you* and *me*. I know what I'm doing about it. Now, what are you going to do about it? Remember, the only thing that allows evil to flourish is that good people do nothing." The one thing that we all can do is pray. We can pray for the children. We can pray for the parents. We can pray for the judges who have to apply the "Wisdom of Solomon." We can pray for ourselves.

I pray for every child that comes into our home. I pray that they may know that they are safe. I pray that they will know that they are loved. I pray that they will experience peace of mind and healing of their spirit. I pray that they will be later placed in a safe, loving home. I pray for protection on their lives. I pray that God will provide them with parents who will not abuse them. I continually pray.

It is interesting to note that every time a social worker comes to our home they say, "You have so many children, however, everything is so peaceful. I just came from a home with far fewer children and it was chaos." We have worked to have a home where love is the foundation and peace reigns and the reason for it is prayer.

Some people are turned off praying because of religion itself. Too often religion is used as an excuse for doing what is wrong, or as a reason for not doing what is right. I understand the frustration people have with religion because I have it as well. I am often shocked and angered at how some Christians will quote and misinterpret the Scripture "Spare the rod and spoil the child" to justify their beating a child with a stick until welts form and blood spills. They will try to rationalize their behaviour by stating, "The hand is for loving, the rod for disciplining." What disgusting rhetoric. Beating a child is wrong at all times and even more criminal when it is done with a stick, and even more so, in the name of God.

Liane and I have, because of our love of children and faith in God, welcomed to our home and hearts, children of every race and religion. It does not matter where the child was born or what "god" their parents worshipped or if their parents worshipped anyone or anything at all. It never enters our minds. We have had children who come from homes whose family have never entered a Church, Synagogue, Temple or Mosque. And we have had children who were born to parents who attend their place of worship regularly. This was never an issue for us. We simply see a child in need. We believe what is most important is that the home that receives these children is loving and stable.

I have become increasingly saddened, as a person of faith and as a Christian, to see people use their religion to justify behaviour that harms children rather than enhances their lives. Whether it is Jehovah's Witness parents who refuse blood transfusions for their child, polygamist Mormons who engage in physical violence against infants, incest or sexual abuse of young girls, extremist Christians who refuse medication or treatment because they believe

God will heal their child, or fundamentalist Muslims who have advocated or turned a blind eye to girls being beaten, mutilated or threatened with death if they have their head or face uncovered in public, that they say dishonors their fathers or families.

One would think that this happens only in other countries and not here in Canada. If that is what you think, you would be wrong. This has happened and is happening; and children have been brought into the care of Children's Aid for their protection for most if not all of these reasons at some point or another.

When the parents of Farah Khan were arrested for her murder and dismemberment I was disgusted, as most were, by the details of how she was callously, continuously and cruelly beaten and abused. Kaneez Fatima, Farah's stepmother, indicated upon arrest that Farah's father, Mohammad Khan, was responsible and that she was not. She suggested that she could not do anything to stop him because she was in an arranged Muslim marriage and a woman can not speak out against her husband because of that and the fear of family reprisals.

I was appalled when he suggested that Farah, a five-year-old, committed suicide by slitting her own throat. The ridiculousness of the suggestion is only surpassed by the shock of his words as he blamed God or Allah for his circumstances. As Jim Coyle quoted him saying in the February 5, 2004 *Toronto Star,* "God, I don't understand what trouble Allah has put me in. I am ruined, I have no one. Please, for God's sake, have pity on me…" Unbelievable!

Even if it is discovered that little Farah Khan did commit suicide – no matter how ludicrous that sounds – and she did so because she could no longer endure living in a world where her life was so abysmal, because the abuse was so brutal, her cries for mercy to her father were unheeded. We must make sure that this can never happen again.

Children ought to have a right to experience life free from

abuse. No one has the right to justify that abuse, or refuse to do anything to stop it because of their faith.

I must admit I can see why people can be turned off by religion in general, and certain religions in particular, after this experience.

The Children's Aid Society seeks to provide safe, culturally and religiously specific homes for the children in their care. They do this because they know that a child needs to feel comfortable in their surroundings in order to recover from the abuse. It is truly important that people come forward to provide these homes. The Children's Aid Society desperately needs Muslim homes, Jewish homes, Christian homes, and homes of every culture and nationality. The priority, however, must always be homes that are places of safety for the child and that can provide for the needs of the child.

This challenge was revealed to us when a baby boy was brought to our home after he was found to have eighteen broken bones and a cracked skull. Like all the children who come through our door, he was unique, a special and precious gift. After many months of care he developed normally and grew quickly.

At one point it was revealed to the parents, by mistake, that I was a minister. Unbeknownst to us or anyone else, the parents, who were Muslim, made an appeal to their Mosque for someone to come forward to take this child because we were Christian. Great pressure came to bear on everyone.

The Children's Aid Society works tirelessly to provide safe homes that take into account the needs and culture of each child. This is not an easy task. Often, there are not homes available to provide for the special culture or religion. In cases like this, the caregivers who have the child seek to make the necessary accommodations regarding diet and traditions for each child. It seems this was not acceptable to the parents or the mosque. A family was found by the parents and the mosque and meetings were set with the Children's Aid Society. Not everyone agreed that moving him was the right or best thing to do.

At one of the meetings, the mother tearfully said to Liane in broken English, "It not you. You loved and cared for my child. I thank you so much. He doing very well. But, my God would not be happy." She then broke down. Liane, understanding her apprehension and fear, took her hand and said, "It's all right. I understand. We are not angry at you. You don't have to be afraid."

I was asked, "What would have been the decision if a committed Christian parent of a child in the care of the Children's Aid Society was demanding that their child be moved because that child was in a Muslim home or some other religion?"

My answer was, "It would be no."

The decision was made that he was to be moved. We were told that the family he was to live with would not enter our home or even come to our home to pick him up for visits because we were Christian. We, not having the same issue, brought him to meet with them. It was a two-week process of short visits that eventually became overnight visits until he finally left our home to live with them.

Things like this can cause one to say, "Why bother?" However, our faith sustains us. The fact is, I have always thought that belief in God is not about adhering to rules and rituals of any given religion, but about developing a relationship with God. Prayer is the means of building that relationship, and developing a mode of communication.

Another reason people don't pray is that they think that prayer is outmoded or old-fashioned. They may think that it is not sophisticated enough for people who live in a scientific age. Others may think that it belongs to the past when superstition and fantasy were seen to answer the questions that were still a mystery. These people believe that prayer and science are incompatible

One of the great ironies, however, is that today the supporters of prayer and proponents of science are engaged in a new and remarkable discussion. In 1997 researchers surveyed American biologists, physicists, and mathematicians about their religious beliefs. They found that 39% believe in God. The interesting thing was that not only did they believe in God, but they believed in the kind of God who answers prayer. The highest percentage of believers in the scientific community was found among mathematicians. These mathematicians practise what many consider the purest kind of science that exists. And yet, they believe in a God who answers prayer.

Along with this, the effects of prayer are being studied by medical scientists. The result of these studies is that they have found that there is compelling evidence of the benefits of prayer, meditation, and relaxation on individuals who pray. The body responds well to prayer. It positively affects cardiovascular, immune, and other systems in healthy ways. What is more interesting is the prayer done by others (intercessory prayer or prayer at a distance) also shows positive effects on the person being prayed for even if the person is unaware of the prayer being offered and is at a great distance from the person praying. What does it mean? It means that prayer changes things. It changes us and others. So don't let religion get in the way of having a relationship with God. Pray every day. Pray for someone in need. Pray for yourself. If you don't feel you have anyone to pray for, pray for me! Pray for my wife and the children. Just pray. Then watch what happens.

Care and share

It was Christmas Eve. We had just returned from the Christmas evening service when the call came.

"Merry Christmas. It's Night Duty. I have a special request."

"O.K. what do you need?"

"I know you only take infant to five-year-olds, but we have a teenager who is pregnant and we have no place anywhere in all of Toronto for her." It was too surreal for words. It was Christmas Eve and I had just become the "Innkeeper." How could I turn "Mary" away? After a brief talk with Liane, I told the worker to bring her along.

"Mary" was 14 and seven months pregnant. Her parents had found out she was pregnant and kicked her out of the house on Christmas Eve! We welcomed her and offered her food and a place to stay. She was the same age as our oldest daughter and became pregnant when she was the same age as our second oldest daughter. It seemed too much to comprehend. Yet, here she was in our home – but there wouldn't be a manger scene for this Mary. Two of our daughters, Sarah and Alyssa, who shared a room together, let her have their room for the night.

The next morning everyone awoke early to share in the opening of their Christmas gifts. Christmas music was playing, the aroma of eggs and bacon cooking sharpened our appetites and everyone was enjoying the spirit of giving. Everyone, except

Mary. Wrapping paper lay everywhere; gifts were piling up around the receivers, and Mary sat quietly at the kitchen table, just watching. When every last gift had been opened, we all thanked each other for the gifts given and received.

It was then that both Sarah and Alyssa noticed that Mary had nothing. She had come, like the infants, with only the clothes on her back. The girls knew that we always bought extra Christmas gifts for children who might come to stay in our home over Christmas. Unfortunately, these gifts were for babies or very young children. We had nothing suitable for a teenager, let alone one who was pregnant. Our daughters spoke quietly to ask permission to give their gifts to Mary. It was easy to reply "Yes." And with tears in our eyes we watched as they gave as a gift what had once been given to them.

The Power of Positive Begging

"Kits for kids" was born that day as a means of providing essential items for every child who came into care with Metro Toronto Social Services Department, not just those who were invited into our home. Since that time, thousands of bags have been made ready to give out to children of all ages who come into care through emergency homes with little more than a diaper and a dirty T-shirt on their backs. Each empty bag is donated by Zellers, and we fill them with age appropriate items like diapers, sanitary wipes, sleepers or pajamas as well as teddy bears, an age-oriented toy and candy, toothbrushes and toothpaste. For the teens we also include gift certificates that we buy from McDonalds, or Burger King or A&W so that if the teenagers end up on the street again, they will at least have a meal or two to see them through their hunger. Someone once asked me how I got the items needed to fill the bags, to which I replied, "It's the power of Positive Begging! What I can't get by asking, I buy myself."

Caring and sharing are essential lessons that we all need to learn and maintain in life. For someone to be a fully realized human being, they must be a person who freely gives, shares and cares. The question that I constantly face is, are we teaching this to our children?

At a Midwestern university an interesting sociological experiment was undertaken with the students being the group under the research microscope. The study focused on sharing and giving. Each student was asked to bring a dime to the next class. There are people starving in India, they were told. There is a plague and they really need help. Those who feel they'd like to give to that country, put the money in an envelope and write on it, "India." They were told that India was far away but there were people in the local area, a family, that really needed groceries to live on now. If they wanted to help these local people it would be given to them anonymously. Place the dime in your envelope and write "poor family" on it. They were then told, "We don't have a photocopier at the school and we badly need to get one. For those who need to copy papers and manuscripts, put your ten cents in the envelope and write 'Copier.'"[1]

Everyone knows that a dime isn't worth very much and can't do very much, even if a thousand students in a university give it. When tallied up, the study found that eighty percent of the money given was contributed to the photocopy machine. They could have chosen to do something to make a real difference, but they didn't. An old Latin proverb applies here, *"Corruptio optimi pessima"* meaning, "The worst corruption is the corruption of the best."

Have we ceased to be concerned with anything and anyone but ourselves? In our work with children, we see a lot of evidence that suggests abuse crosses all class, racial and cultural lines. I have discovered, though, that a disproportionate amount of those children who come into our care come from homes that suffer from one or all of the cluster of troubles of poverty, unemployment, addiction and mental health issues. It is not just an issue of bad or inadequate parenting. The mental and physical roots of abuse have as much to do with the lack of social and cultural support systems as they do with the lack of psychological well-being. It is an issue of nurture, nature, culture and society. When we are focusing only on the psychological reasons for child abuse we fail to address the societal causes and criminal consequences.

Child poverty continues to be an increasing problem in Canada and the United States. Research shows:

- Poor children are more likely to have low birth weights resulting in adverse effects such as chronic illness and disabilities;
- Poor children are more likely to have lower functioning vision, hearing, speech, mobility, dexterity, cognition, emotion and pain/discomfort;
- Poor children are less likely to participate in organized sports and recreational activities;
- Poor children are less likely to live in safe neighbourhoods and are at a disproportionate risk of exposure to environmental contaminants.
- Despite improvements in the economy through the late 1990s, child poverty rates across the country have not been reduced. Between 1989 and 1998 the number of children who were poor nearly doubled in Canada from 247,000 to 471,500 in those years. Almost one in five children in Canada is raised in poverty.

The research has also shown that:

"Child abuse is strongly related to class, inequality and poverty both in terms of prevalence and severity. Locating the problem in terms of social structural factors has important implications for the way we define the problem, the way we explain it and the best way of doing something about it. For solving the problem requires a realignment in social policy which recognizes the necessity of attacking the social, economic and cultural conditions associated with abuse."[2]

Beyond the societal problems there is also the criminal issue, which is often not addressed because of the focus on the psychological roots of abuse. The violence perpetrated against children is a criminal activity. The violence against children is often considered a form of child mismanagement or a mistaken view of discipline rather than what in fact it is – a crime. This is how we once viewed domestic violence against women. For years violence against women was justified as simply being a domestic problem not a criminal action. It is because of the work of enlightened legislators that this is no longer the case.

The consequence of this undue focus on the psychological rather than social/environmental and criminal aspects of child abuse is that the child is bounced from the abusive family home into the foster care system and, when things appear to cool down, back to the family home where the abuse continues, and they're forced to take refuge in another foster home.

The environmental and social issues can not be addressed by social workers because it is a matter for the government. As a result, the focus remains on a response providing only a limited therapeutic bandage.

The Court also continues with the mindset that it is a child-rearing problem and the tennis game continues with the child as the ball being batted back and forth until the damage is so serious and the cycle so ingrained in the child's psyche that as they mature and become an adult and have children of their own the abuse is most assuredly to be passed on.

Often years pass before a judge will decide when there is

enough evidence to sever the parental rights. Yet by this time the child is either too old or too damaged to be adopted. The result is that the child is raised by the CAS and often bounced around for the rest of their childhood, unless a family commits to raising her or him until they become a legal adult. I can only hope they have been able to steer clear of seeking solace with a local gang, a sure road to failure and jail.

The judge, rather than determining the abuse as a crime and severing the relationship, looks at the extenuating circumstances and sends the child home to be abused again. It isn't rocket science. A child who has multiple broken bones and cigarette burns should never be returned to the home where it occurred. However, the old view, and I have many reasons to disbelieve the adage, "blood being thicker than water," still remains.

That is why it is so important that there are loving people who will open their hearts and homes to care and share their love with these little ones.

Children require people who will teach them with love that they are amazing, magical, miracles of God. They need to be shown how to love and be loved, to have compassion and be compassionate. Everyone assumes that as individuals they will get this along the way. And then we wonder why children are killing children. We wonder why teens will shoot pellet guns for kicks or to show off, through car windows at women and children, maiming, disfiguring, and disabling their victims for life. Everyone assumes that these twisted children will somehow learn along the way that they should treat people with dignity and humanity. Yet, we don't realize children learn what they see. If their life is filled with violence, abuse and abandonment, is it really any surprise that is how they will live?

The sad reality of the work that we do with CAS is that we are starting to see the *children of the children* who came into our emergency home twelve years ago arrive into our present home now. Is the cycle of violence, drug and alcohol abuse, and abandonment doomed to continue to move through still another generation? Our only consolation is that we know that there have been those fortunate children who have been saved from this roundabout of abuse and are living in loving homes and have the potential for productive lives.

Children Learn What They Live and Then Live Out What They Have Learned

We model for our children how to live life with us every day and into their future. The only question is, what kind of model do we present? Can we expect children to become people who care and share, when all they've lived within is an atmosphere of abuse and selfishness? How can we expect our children to be responsible and loving unless we live our lives setting the example of responsibility and doing it lovingly? What they observe will become their patterns and values.

We must become living models who teach our children that they are unique, wonderful human beings created and entrusted by God, worthy to be treated with care, compassion, dignity and humanity.

In one of the Children's Aid Medical Clinics where we bring the children for intake medicals there hangs a poem that speaks profoundly to this point.

Children Learn What They Live

If a child lives with criticism, he learns to condemn.
If a child lives with hostility, she learns to fight.
If a child lives with ridicule, he learns to be shy.
If a child lives with shame, she learns to be guilty.
If a child lives with tolerance, he learns to be patient.
If a child lives with encouragement, she learns confidence.
If a child lives with praise, he learns to appreciate.
If a child lives with fairness, she learns justice.
If a child lives with security, he learns to have faith.
If a child lives with approval, she learns to like herself.
If a child lives with acceptance and friendship,
    he learns to find love in the world.

---

1 Buscaglia, L., *Living, Loving and Learning*, New York,
New York: Holt, Rinehart and Winston, 1982

2 Corby, Brian, *Child Abuse, Towards a Knowledge Base*, Open University Press,
(Buckingham, copyright 2000) p.149

Remember to say "Thank-you"

She came to us late one night from "Sick Kids Hospital." The social worker that accompanied her was in tears as he told us of some of the infant's injuries. Saddie was six months old, yet she looked as if she was recently born. A few months should make a big difference in a child's development. It didn't in her case. She was tragically small, thin and emaciated. She weighed less that day than she had at her birth six months earlier. She had a cast on one arm. The social worker asked us to return her to the hospital on Monday for a full skeletal x-ray to find the extent of her injuries.

While trying to feed her from a bottle over the weekend, we found that she had never learned how to suck. For three days we squeezed formula into her little mouth like a bird does for her young, until she learned to suck normally from a nipple. At the hospital it was discovered that she had more multiple bone fractures. We brought her home and very carefully began the work of helping her to heal physically, and almost more importantly, emotionally.

Tenderly, we would hold her fractured body as we fed her baby formula. Initially, we were only able to feed her half an ounce at a time. This meant that she would require multiple feedings throughout the day and night until her little body became accustomed to having more. This meant many sleepless nights. Eventually, her ability to drink more grew from half an ounce at a time to an ounce and a half, and then two and then four ounces. At this point, her feeding schedule was every three hours. Her sleep was fitful and restless. Each time she would squirm – as infant's do – she would scream, due to the pain it would cause. We gently gathered her in our arms, taking turns comforting her, until she again returned to the blissfulness of sleep tucked in the crook of our arm. As I held her, her head would often rest peacefully on my left shoulder and against my neck. The rhythm of my breathing and the beating of my heart seemed to soothe her. On some level she knew instinctively she was safe and loved.

Children have an incredible will to live. They have an amazing inborn strength to overcome the obstacles that confront them. As Liane worked with the doctors, nurses and physiotherapists to help this little child, I was constantly amazed at how she had the will to overcome every obstacle. I would sit in amazement also at the stamina of Liane who never wavered in her desire to help this child and all the children we have had become well. Day after day, Liane would sit on the floor in the living room going through the program of physiotherapy that was set out for Saddie by the physiotherapist. Each week when the therapist came to our home she saw the improvement made as a result of Liane's amazing care.

At first we saw Saddie change through tears and later with a miracle of giggles. Surprising what a little love and a lot of work can do. We watched as day by day and week by week she overcame her every obstacle. Soon she grew to be healthy and strong. Months passed and the day came when she moved away to be raised by a wonderful family with the hope of her being adopted by them if the courts allowed.

Life is filled with such wonders. A little infant arrives with a traumatized and broken body, shattered spirit, and uncertain future, and leaves whole, healthy, and with the hope of a bright future in a loving home. A comment from G.K. Chesterton is so appropriate: "The world will never starve for want of wonders, but for want of wonder."

The lesson is clear. There is much that is horrible, even outrageous in life, but we are able to live in a wonderful world because there are people who want to do wonders that make it so. People like the couple who had committed to love, care, raise and adopt Saddie, and who gave us much to be grateful for as they made a place in their hearts and home for this wonderful little girl.

Yet, it is so easy to take things for granted. We live in a free country. We are well fed. We have a roof over our head, and money in our pockets. It's true, we might not be as well off as some, but compared to most of the world we are rich. We are not only blessed materially, we are blessed with friends, family, and a future. But, in spite of all this, we are sometimes slow to acknowledge our blessings. This may be because we have grown so accustomed to them, we take them for granted – and it's easy to do. Occasionally we need a little jog to be reminded of just what we have been taking for granted, and to acknowledge what we have to make us thankful.

When Rudyard Kipling was England's most popular writer in late 19th and early 20th centuries, the word went out that his publishers paid him a dollar a word for his work. Some Cambridge students, hearing of this, cabled Kipling one dollar, along with the instructions: "Please send us one of your very best words." Kipling replied with a one-word telegram: "Thanks." The word "thanks" is one of the very best words, worth much to the person who speaks it and to the person who hears it. It is expressed so well in the Bible: "A word fitly spoken is like apples of gold in a setting of silver." (Prov. 25:11)

Thanks is indeed a fitly spoken word. But too often it is left unspoken. What we need to cultivate is an attitude of gratitude. The reason is simple. We live in an era of ingratitude. Aristotle recognized this when he said, "What soon grows old? Gratitude."

She ran down the stairs and threw her tiny four-year-old arms around my leg, and said, "Thank-you."

"For what?" I asked.

"For letting me stay here." Then she skipped off to play.

"Thank-you," I replied to myself.

Thank-you for reminding me of why I do this, I thought.

Thank-you for reminding me I am blessed.

Thank-you for reminding me that I am to be a blessing.

Why are there so many complainers? I heard of a recent medical survey which stated that chronic complainers live longer than people who are always sweet and serene. It claims that their cantankerous spirit gives them a purpose for living. Each morning they get up with a fresh challenge to see how many things they can find to grumble about, and they derive great satisfaction from making others miserable. Do you suppose this is true? I doubt it. It seems to me that it is questionable whether those who complain actually do outlive those who don't. Maybe because of their discomfort, it just seems that way to everybody around them.

There are many benefits to cultivating an attitude of gratitude. Perhaps the greatest is that giving thanks has a powerful effect on our lives. It changes us. The act of giving thanks makes us different.

It is true that we live in an ungrateful age. Look around you. Daily you will see people who are bitter. Is it not true that "Some people are bitter, not because they do not have *anything*, but because they do not have *everything*." We have been well taught to be greedy and grasping. We are bombarded by commercials that remind us of what we do not have. Holidays like Christmas become a depressing time for many. We are led to believe that if we do not have things we will not experience happiness. And so we are unhappy people.

Unhappy people may be said to be unthankful people. At first glance, you may think them unthankful because they are unhappy. That is not true. In fact, the opposite is true. They are not unthankful because they are unhappy, but they are unhappy because they are unthankful.

The act of giving thanks has the power to transform us into different people. We will not only be different from the people around us, we will also be different from the way we used to be. We will be transformed. We will be transformed in our thinking and in our temperament. As we seek to cultivate this attitude of gratitude, our thinking will be transformed because we will begin to program our minds to think in a different way. The way of the world is to concentrate on the negative. Our tendency is to correct and to point out errors or omissions. But the way of God is to emphasize the positive. We are to look for the good in everything. We can find the negative when we look for it. We can also find the positive when we look for it. So why not be happy and seek out the positive? Why wouldn't that be easier to sustain?

For instance, someone said, "We can be thankful that husbands try to repair things around the house." They usually make things worse and the problem big enough to call in professionals. We can be thankful for children who clean up what they mess up. They're such a joy you hate to send them home to their parents. We can be thankful for smoke alarms. They tell us when the chicken's done. There is always a positive side. As we choose to think on it, our minds will be transformed.

Matthew Henry, the famous scholar, had such an occasion. He was once accosted by thieves and robbed of his wallet. He entered these words in his diary:

Let me be thankful first, because I was never robbed before; second, because, although they took my purse, they did not take my life; third, because, although they took my all, it was not much; and fourth, because it was I who was robbed, not I who robbed.

This is evidence of a man who had a transformed temperament and transformed thinking. His life had been changed by choosing to be thankful. This choice will enable all of us to move forward in many other areas. Cicero advised, "A thankful heart is not only the greatest virtue, but the parent of all other virtues."

For four decades East Berlin was controlled by the Communists. West Berlin was free. One day people who lived in East Berlin took a truckload of garbage and dumped it on the West Berlin side. The people of West Berlin could have retaliated by doing the same thing. But instead they took a truckload of canned goods, bread, and milk and neatly stacked it on the East Berlin side. On top of this stack of food they placed the sign, "Each gives what he has."

Say, "I'm sorry"

A little girl from the neighbourhood said in a moment of anger and insensitivity to our daughter Tabitha, "Why don't you go back to your mother who is black instead of staying with your white mommy and daddy." Tabitha was shattered and shaken. For nearly six months she was tormented. She didn't tell us of the incident; however, her behaviour spoke volumes. She became withdrawn and angry. At school there was an amazing older Jamaican lady who volunteered in her kindergarten class and at recess. Tabitha would run to her and give her a big hug and kiss. She adored her, as did we. A few months after the incident with the neighbour the dear lady took Liane aside and showed her the scratches and bruises that Tabitha was making on this lady's arm. Rather, than hugging and kissing, she was kicking and scratching. Liane took Tabitha aside and told her that she had to say she was sorry. She did. We asked her, "Why did you do such a thing?"

She said, "She is black and I hate her." We knew that something was wrong. She went on to tell us about the incident with the neighbour and then said, "I don't want to be brown. I want to be white like you. Why did you adopt me? I want to be with my black mother."

She was so confused and angry and hurt. She began to weep. We told her as gently as possible that we loved her and would always love her. We reminded her that we loved her just the way

God made her, "Beautiful and Carmel," as she used to call herself. We also told her that even if it was possible – and it wasn't – for her to be with her birth mother, she needed to know that she was white, and that her birth father was black.

The next day we went to the school and explained what had happened to her teacher and the assistant. Mrs. Wakefield, her teacher, was truly wonderful. She gave us a children's book entitled *Beautiful Brown* and told us that we could have it for as long as we needed it. She took extra special care with Tabitha in her class. We will forever be grateful to the both of them for this.

The book spoke of loving yourself as the colour God made you. The little girl in the book looked just like Tabitha, "Beautiful Brown." We read it to her every night and whenever she wanted to hear it again. As we did we hugged her and kissed her before, during and after. Every time it said, "Beautiful Brown," we would say, "That's you!" and hug her. She would giggle and squeal. It took some time, but she was able to go back to that little girl that hurt her – who later became her friend – no longer feeling inferior and say, with self-respect and dignity, "I forgive you, but you need to know that this is my mommy and daddy and I am beautiful brown whether you like it or not."

Forgiveness is never free. It seems strange to say this; but it is true. It always costs someone something. That is why it is so very difficult to forgive. That is also why it is so difficult for people to move on from their past to claim their future.

Martin Luther King, Jr. fought to live in a country free from racism, where people will "no longer be judged by the colour of their skin but by the content of their character." Nelson Mandela was imprisoned for 25 years for his fight against Apartheid and for freedom. They understood that freedom is never free.

Just as freedom is never free, so forgiveness is never free. And true freedom comes through forgiveness.

Forgiveness always costs someone something. It is also why

some never forgive. These are the people who never move beyond that moment in time when the evil was done, or pain inflicted. Life around them moves on, time moves on, they don't. They live out of that moment in time, whether they admit it or not. They react to everything and everyone around them out of the emotions of that moment in the past. For a person to be able to move on in their lives they must forgive or forever be in bondage to the past.

Forgiveness is *recognition* that the painful, sinful and perhaps even evil event happened. It is a *declaration* that what happened should never have happened. It gives *confirmation* and in some sense *condemnation* of how wrong it was *before* it offers *redemption*.

When we forgive, the act of forgiveness itself confirms that what happened deserves condemnation, yet we choose redemption. Forgiveness is claiming the power over the problem and redeeming it for a purpose. It is the taking back of that moment. It is a cleansing. It is whipping away of the pus of bitterness and replacing it with the anointing of forgiveness. It is an act that can bring about *reconciliation*. Forgiveness gives the victim freedom. Forgiveness gives control to the victim and gives them the ability to become the victor. Reconciliation also can bring freedom to the one who has done the victimizing. It all depends on our willingness to release the bitterness in favour of forgiveness.

A captive was once brought before King James II of England. The King reprimanded the prisoner: "Don't you know that it is in my power to pardon you?" The scared, shaking prisoner replied, "Yes, I know it is in your power to pardon me, but it is not in your nature."

Forgiveness does seem at times beyond our natural ability. It is easier to seek revenge than reconciliation. However, it is not beyond God's ability to intervene and help us do so. There are some things that are beyond our control. There are some things that are beyond our power. Yet, these are not beyond our control, if we allow God to intervene in our lives and bring about cleansing and healing.

Hatred and bitterness can bind us to the past; but forgiveness can free us for the future. Forgiveness is not so much *for* the other person (who has hurt you) but for you. The person who has hurt you leaves you to continue to hurt yourself through bitterness and self-abuse. Even if the other person does not ask for, or accept your forgiveness; you need to give it for your personal and spiritual well-being.

Forgiveness frees us. It frees us to love and be loved, to be and become. Without forgiveness, walls of bitterness are built that cannot be penetrated by anyone or anything. These walls get higher and thicker over time until the loneliness and alienation become too much to bear. It is for this reason that we teach all our children that it is important to say "I'm sorry." We have seen the destructive results of a life of bitterness and broken lives.

Every day we see children enslaved by the pain of their past, enraged by the exploitation, and broken by abuse as they thrash about in self-destructive ways. At times they come into our home angry and hurting, kicking, and fighting against being there; yet hoping and praying inside that it will be a safe place for them and their younger baby sister or brother.

Johnny and his baby sister Susie came to us after being picked up off the street. He couldn't stand the chaos of living in a violent and dangerous crack house anymore. He took his baby sister and left. Johnny was a very mature four-year-old. Imagine being four and deciding that you have had enough and you have to get your baby sister out of the place where you are living. Imagine the fear, and anger, that would be in a constant swirl within you.

Johnny and his sister arrived in the early evening, dirty and hungry. We fed and cleaned them up and got them ready for bed. After we put Susie down, we decided that we would move our daughter Tabitha out of her room and let Johnny occupy it for the evening. We wanted him to be close by, within earshot so that we could hear if there were any problems. He was not happy when we put him to bed and began kicking, fighting and screaming. He was a volcano of anger. He kicked against the walls and anything else he could get to. We were not concerned about damage as it was a childproof room. There were toys if he wanted to play. We said good-night and left him to go to sleep. Then I heard the crash of shattering glass. I ran into the room to find him hanging out the window trying to make his escape. He had shattered the entire frame. I grabbed him by the leg to keep him inside as I removed his shirt to look for the cuts I was sure would be there. There were none. He was fine, but my window was another matter.

Luckily, I have a very good friend, Doug Morris of Morris Glass, whose company installs windows. I called him. He had just returned from his cottage. He arrived at our home at 11:00 p.m., secured a temporary replacement and took measurements to have a new heavy-duty window installed. He was gone by 1:00 a.m. By then Johnny had already gone to sleep in my bed with Liane watching over him. He nestled into my arms as I carried him into his own bed.

In the morning, Lynn, our three-and-a-half-year-old who had been with us since birth, came in and saw the damage. She looked at Johnny and said, "Say sorry." He just growled. She looked shocked. Lifting her hands in an expression of confusion and exasperation she looked at me with raised eyebrows, "No sorry? How be happy, if no sorry?"

Even at three and a half, Lynn knew that you can't be happy if you don't say the magic word "sorry."

What you mess up, clean up

We have a very simple rule in our house. "What you mess up – you clean up." When our own children were very young and we had other children in our home, we would sing a little song that we learned somewhere. It was a song that called everyone to come and help clean up the mess that was made.

> *"Clean up, Clean up, everybody do their share.*
> *Clean up, Clean up, everything and everywhere."*

We reminded the children before we did this that if they made a mess, they had to clean it up before going on to play or do something else. They were made responsible for doing it properly, too. When they were very young, we did it for them as they often stood by to watch. As they grew, we set the standard as we helped them with the chores, and still later, when they were to do it for themselves.

It is a lesson that makes life easier when we understand that we are all responsible for the lives we live, for the messes we make. The Greek philosopher Heraclitus who was known for his brilliant and provocative sayings 2,500 years ago said it this way, "Your character is your destiny." An amazing statement! It means that everything that is happening around you is happening because of who you are. You are where you are because of who you are. Our destinies are determined through the various decisions we make, and the actions we take or choose not to take on a daily basis. It means that you are responsible.

A poem comes to mind that my mother used when I was in trouble. It frightened me almost to death. It still, at times, leaves me feeling unsettled. However, today I use it as a reminder of how to replace harmful habits with beneficial ones.

> Sow a thought, reap an act,
> Sow an act, reap a habit,
> Sow a habit, reap character,
> Sow a character, reap a destiny.

There is a fine edge to the poem that clings to you as it builds each line in importance. It cuts both ways. It says that we reap what we sow, and what goes around surely comes around. It tells us that our thoughts lead to actions and our actions lead to consequences that can have a lasting effect on our lives and future and the lives of others.

Every day I see parents who have to deal with the consequences of their behaviour. Sadness arrives when we discover that most don't learn from their mistakes.

Joan has 17 children. Every one is being cared for by Children's Aid. Yet, rather then doing what she needs to do to get her life in order and her children back, her response is, "You can take them, but I can make them." What provokes a person to make such an outrageous, irresponsible, unsocial statement? The truth is she can and mostly likely will have more children. She is in her late 30s, and has quite a few childbearing years ahead of her. She refuses to change her behaviour and she and her children continue to pay the price for her refusal. Is it anger, spite, despair that drives her to this form of social madness? Do social workers stand at the bottom of the bed of her delivery room and catch each child and whisk it away to safety in a foster home? The answer is most likely "Yes" to both questions. If she chooses not to change then it is the job of the social workers to protect the child. When the social workers hear of another pregnancy the hospital is notified to watch for her arrival. When she arrives at the hospital the workers are notified to come and apprehend the child. It is a sad reality of life. Is there an answer that will stop this foolhardiness?

And what of the children who die due to their parents' neglect or abuse? What are we doing about them? I think of the cases of baby Jordan who was starved to death by his self-absorbed mother who later blamed society for the death of her baby as she walked from the court house laughing, smiling, smoking and without serving any jail time for his murder. And Sara Podniewicz whose cracked-addicted parents killed her through their neglect and abuse. I think of baby Sara Cao who lived for only 39 days, the last three of which were on life support. She had 10 fractured ribs. Some of the broken ribs were old injuries and were not caused by the final brutal and violent abuse that ultimately killed her.

What did the judge do in this case? Judge Fairgrieve slapped her on the wrist and sent her home without having to serve "the usual house arrest and community service provisions," believing that Ms Cao had had to endure enough during her 22 days in custody between her arrest and release on bail. He did this, he told her, so that he would not "add to your misery."

According the Christie Blatchford, a reporter for the *Globe and Mail*, and a champion for the protection of children, Judge Fairgrieve praised the prosecutors for the plea bargain that got Ms Cao off "for having made a more reasonable and enlightened assessment of the public interest." He went on to say, "A segment of the community would no doubt take the view that any offence involving the death of a helpless infant at the hands of her inadequate and violent mother should result in substantial imprisonment." He obviously was of the enlightened kind that didn't believe this. I am not. Murder is murder; whether it is done *to* a mother of a child or *by* the mother *to* the child. The Judge, lawyers, and the prosecutors should be ashamed of themselves for making this plea bargain.

If it had been an adult woman, and not a baby girl who had been assaulted and died as a result of "blunt force trauma to the head," the person who had done this would be in jail, and rightfully so. Yet, a murder of a baby is of no consequence and deserves none. This Judge made that perfectly clear.

Police Detective Constable Andy Gibson said in shock to the sentence, "I feel like there's no justice for this five-week-old baby... no one will remember her now."

I wish the prosecutors and judges were required to get up at three in the morning with my wife and me and see these children when they come into our care with their clothes covered in blood and vomit after being bandaged at the hospital. I wish they were required to come with us to "Sick Kids" as the doctors and nurses, hardened after years of seeing everything, weep as they try, with our help, to get a skeletal scan while the baby screams in agony because of injuries. Perhaps then they would see the need for justice for children and that deterrence against abuse is a justifiable reason to sentence an adult to jail for injuring or murdering their child. Excusing someone for murder because they had a hard upbringing, or only "managed to scrape through Grade 12" suggests that anyone who has had a hard life ought to be able to murder anyone they like and get away with it.

There are thousands of parents who have experienced hellish childhoods, and who are not exactly "bright"; yet they don't pick up their child and murder them or leave them to starve to death. Judges like Judge Fairgrieve, and the prosecutors Anna Tenhouse and Rebecca Edwards, may indeed be fine people but it appears they are blinded by the cloak of sympathy to what true justice is. Perhaps they ought to be sentenced to upgrading their humanity by doing community service at a shelter for abused women and children so that they can see how they are enabling this abuse to continue, and participating in the abuse themselves by allowing it to continue.

It is time to clean up this mess. It is time to stop this idiocy. It is time that we, as a society and we as individuals get out of our own way and clean this up.

Get Out of Your Own Way

One of the main reasons we don't get what we want in life is because we get in our own way. We hinder or hold ourselves back from getting what we truly want out of life because of habits, behaviours, addictions that recur almost daily. We can't help but get in our own way, where we step on our own feet. We continue to repeat old behaviour patterns that result in negative consequences and stifled ambition throughout our present and future. Yet, we don't want to take responsibility for these actions, habits, behaviours that probably could be better described as addictions.

The truth is we remain responsible whether we like it or not. The problem is created when we choose not to take responsibility and try to move it somewhere else. And what we need to realize is that there is no failure in life, except the failure to take responsibility for our actions. It is very easy to ignore responsibilities today. It has become so very easy to put the blame on others. I recently heard of a person who won a multi-million dollar lawsuit after getting lung cancer. This person stated in response to the award, "Well, if I develop lung cancer from smoking, it's not my fault. I blame the cigarette companies, and they need to pay." This person failed to accept any responsibility for his ailment from a destructive habit. It is true that the cigarette companies are responsible. However, that doesn't remove the person's individual responsibility for protecting their health.

As a society, we have become too adept at blaming others and excusing ourselves as pseudo-innocents – too easily victimized. Some people blame heredity, environment, chemical imbalance, job pressures, poverty, prejudices, abuse, their upbringing and anything else they can reach for to lay the blame for their problems. Many reasons may in fact be valid. The only question is do you want a reason or results?

The Choice is Yours

A story circulated several years ago about twin sisters who had an alcoholic mother. One sibling became an alcoholic, and the other a total abstainer. When the alcoholic was asked why, she said, "Well, my mother was an alcoholic, so what can you expect?" When the other was asked why she chose to become a total abstainer she said, "Well, my mother was an alcoholic, so what can you expect?" Same answer but such a different application.

The choice becomes yours. You can choose to be better than your heredity or environment or you can choose to use a worthless crutch as an excuse to limp through an imperfect life. Do you want reasons or results? Do you want a reason to remain the same? Do you want a reason to never change? Why would you want a reason to stay in the same quicksand of misery, sinking deeper every time you move? You can always find a reason for seeking secure ground. Do you want to change the end result that your life is headed for? If you do, there is a way to do it.

Choose a life: will it be self-destruction, or will you raise yourself to seek self-improvement and with it achieve self-empowerment? Everyone is in the same boat. You can play the game or lay the blame. What will it be? Winner or loser?

Blaming or Accepting

From the earliest days in my counselling practice I found that many people make the choice to play the blame game. They say things like, "It's not my fault that things are the way they are and my life is as it is. Why should I bother doing anything to seek change? I didn't cause things to happen the way they are. It's not my fault; it's someone else's."

One of the main reasons many people never succeed in life is they can't pry themselves out of the blame game. It's controlling and condemning the participant to play on a field where no one can win. Failure to accept responsibility is truly one of the greatest failures.

"Your character is your destiny." Everything that is happening is bound to happen because of who you have chosen to become. You are where you are because of *who* you are. Our destinies are determined through the various decisions we make on a daily basis. It is no one's fault but our own that we are surrounded by the particular environment we find ourselves in. We make, or choose to avoid making, certain decisions. We pay attention to one thing and ignore another that is often better. We decide what time to go to bed and how late we will sleep in. We decide how hard we will work or how much leisure time we will take. No one forces you to watch five hours of television at night while someone else works hard on a new business deal. Your character does determine your destiny.

You may say, "That may be true but I didn't choose the awful thing that was done to me." You would be right, but only you can choose to remain mired in the quicksand of a failure. However, we can choose how we will respond to that awful event in our life. In doing so, we choose our destiny in relation to that event. By making any given decision we can determine the direction our life will take – at least for a time. If we do this often enough over a period of time, our decisions determine our direction, and then our direction determines our destination and destiny.

Character is created and shaped by the many varied influences in our lives. Our character consists of how we develop our basic natural and human instincts. These instincts are shaped by our family, upbringing, and value systems. They are shaped by our education, culture, and by the events of our lives that are often set in play by our friends or colleagues. Over time our character is developed.

At one time, a person's character was thought to be important enough to focus attention on when determining their place in society. People spent time working on and protecting their character so they would be declared virtuous. Today, most people simply allow it to develop without much thought as to how it is developing or to be developed in the first place. They give hardly a second's thought to the things they are allowing to influence them. When things go badly, because of our poor judgment, we too often blame others, our circumstances or society. Such a reckless, easy out so we don't have to take responsibility!

Reasons or Results

Blaming others or elements of society for our life situation helps no one. You have a choice. Blame and shame others for your life situation and make up reasons why things are not going well. Or you can accept responsibility, move on and get results. Do you want reasons or results? That is the question you must ask of yourself and your standards if all you want is reasons for the way you are so you can stay the way you are. Easy. People will always find reasons to stay the way they are. If, however, there is a desire for progress and results, they must start to look at their life and begin to accept responsibility for the decisions that have to be made. Take the ladder necessary to change the direction you want your life to take. Just raise your foot to the first rung, push off and start to climb. No one can do it for you. For you are where you are because of who you are.

One of the most devastating lies we tell ourselves is contained in four small words, "I am a victim."

When we choose to accept no responsibility for our destiny we fail to see reality. We seem to love being victims in our society. To be sure, there are victims of random acts of violence. There are those who are innocently assaulted, robbed and killed every day. However, selecting yourself as being a victim is very much an attitude. We can be victimized, but that doesn't make us a victim. The first means that something was done to a person, the other defines the person. Once we define ourselves as victims we lose all ability to choose our destiny. We give the power to victimizers, criminals, society, bureaucrats and outside structures. We give them the power to define us as victims and thereby control us! It may be true that what was done to us is not our fault. However, what we later choose to do with what was done to us is very much under our control.

Victim or Victor

Victor Frankl tells of how, while in a Nazi concentration camp during World War II, everything was taken away from him. He watched as people gave up and died. He said that the Nazis could take everything away from him except one thing – his right to choose how he would respond.

That right is also yours – to choose how you will respond to the world around you and to your inner world. No one can take that right away from you. No one can make you a victim unless you allow it. And if you let them, you need to face the fact that you are choosing and giving in to be a victim. You choose to accept their definition of your life. You create and put the chains around your ankles.

A woman has the right to choose how she will respond to the rapist, or the murderer of a family member. You have the right to choose how you will respond to your family, the ills of society, the abusive parent, or spouse, or rebellious child. You are not a victim of society, unless you surrender and allow yourself to be.

Marcus Aurelius was so very astute: "If you are pained by an external thing, it is not the thing that disturbs you, but your own judgment about it. And it is in your power to wipe this out now."

He was right. You have it within your power to make the pain stop. You have it within your power to stop being a victim. Solomon said in his proverbs (23:7), "For as a man thinketh in his heart, so is he."

Too many people in their heart of hearts believe themselves to be victims. They accept that definition all too readily. Part of the reason is because it appears to be safe. It means that others have to take care of you. It means you do not have to take responsibility for your future or your life. However, the result is that you allow yourself to become powerless. But you are not powerless. That is a lie! Don't believe it, don't surrender to it! You are more powerful then you think, or can possibly imagine.

Be Bitter or Become Better

Many people embrace the excuse that life isn't the way it should be to stop themselves from becoming all they could be. The cry of every child and the child within every adult is: "IT'S NOT FAIR!" That may be true, but that happens to be what life offers. Life *is* not fair. It never has been. It never will be. We may wish it to be, but it isn't. That doesn't make it right or wrong. It just is.

The problem is that when we were children we were taught that life should be fair. Fairness was taught in school and at home. When playing games, we were told to be fair. When cutting pies, we were told that everything had to be even. Life isn't even, or equal – or fair. We must continue to believe that it must be good in principle to strive to make it fair. However, the truth remains – it isn't fair. And when we try to apply this measure of fairness to every situation we are left in distress and anger.

Life isn't easy. It isn't fair. Knowing this will help you choose to become better instead of bitter. When we believe that everything should be fair we begin to become bitter when we discover it isn't. Some, as a result, use that as an excuse to give up. It isn't fair that a young person is killed in a drive-by shooting, or by a drunk driver. It isn't fair that a person with less experience or qualifications got the job. And you didn't get it because they knew someone higher up. It isn't fair that children are abused or born to crack-addicted mothers. It isn't fair that the laws seem to do nothing about it. It just isn't fair. But that's what life has mapped out for us to live within.

You can live the lie, get angry and give up. Or you can accept the truth, get steady on your feet and set your body and mind to do something worthwhile. You can plan and take action to do something to make it better, or you can just sulk and remain bitter.

MADD was created by one such woman who wanted to bring something good out of a bad situation. She got mad after the automobile death of her child and created Mothers Against Drunk Driving.

My wife and I continued to be angered at the situation of children being born to crack and heroin addicted mothers with ruined spirits and lack of true maternal values and the damage done to them and their children in the ensuing years due to the lack of help offered. We became angry at the fact of abuse against the most vulnerable of all children. As a result we decided to get up and do something about it. We were both trained in social work so we decided to open our home to these damaged children. Life isn't fair. Don't get bitter; set your mind and practise to become better.

"Life Should Be Easy – Wrong"

We live in a society that believes in ease. We have dishwashers, microwaves, garage door openers, central heating, air-condi-tioning and central vacuum cleaning. We have all these things in the desire to make life easier. Well, is it better? We have become so used to a life of fast food and easy living that when hard times hit (and they always do) the illusion of ease evaporates like the mist it portrays and leaves us in despair.

It is wonderful that we are so privileged to have these modern acquisitions. However, you've seen that what often is a blessing can become a curse when the money is tight. Everyone strives to minimize the pain and maximize the pleasure in life. But life isn't easy. In *The Road Less Traveled*, by Scott Peck, he says, "Life is difficult ... Once we truly know that life is difficult – once we truly understand and accept it – then life is no longer difficult."

Bernie Siegal reports, "One can not get through life without pain. What we can do is choose how to use the pain life presents to us."

No Pain No Gain

There is no gain without pain. It's an old sports adage. Have we begun to understand that everything that is worth something costs something? Body builders have always known this. They know that pain produces gain.

I personally discovered this after I had lost 100 pounds. With the fat I lost, I also lost muscle. I lost so much muscle that I felt I would lose an arm-wrestling match with my oldest daughter, who was ten at the time. As a result I joined a gym, learned about nutrition and worked out in balance. I discovered that the pain to achieve better mental an physical condition can be productive. I was told that if I didn't hurt over the next few days after working out, I had not worked out hard enough, stopped too soon. Pain became a measure of success to me. During my trips to exercise I discovered that others were also in pain. We laughed at how hard it ached to walk having worked over the muscles in our legs two days earlier. And then we would dig in and work out our backs and shoulders. Pain was a measure of success. We realized that everything that is worth achieving costs something.

Choose Fear or Faith

We must all move on so we can turn from blaming to accepting, from being bitter to becoming better, from pain to gain, and fear to faith.

There is a choice that every one of us has – live in fear, or live in freedom. Live for that which is temporal and temporary and forever fear losing it. Or live for that which is eternal and know the fullness of God's grace.

Ernest Hemingway, every January, would give away things that he owned. They were important to him, not the unimportant trivia that one might put in a garage sale. He said that he gave them away because "I wanted to know that I possessed them and not that they possessed me." Some of us are possessed by the things we have, whether they be our material possessions, jobs, spouses, children or our addictions. Sadly, Hemingway never gave away the two things he needed to give away that possessed him until the end – alcohol and the gun that caused his suicide.

Jean-Paul Sartre had a less noble reason to give things away. He gave things away so that, "Others and not he, would be possessed by them."

There are no failures, only lessons

> *The reason I know so much is because*
> *I have made so many mistakes.*
> *~ R. Buckminster Fuller*

Caring and learning with children has caused me to *unlearn* a great deal that people taught me. I'm having to get rid of all the garbage fed to me over the years. To my great delight, the more I discard the freer I become.

One of the lessons I learned very early on, and that I continue to unlearn, is that in life there are failures. The truth is in life there are NO failures. And this is one of my greatest truths that I learned from watching many children interact – there are no failures, only lessons.

Why would we teach our children that they are failures? Learning has nothing to do with passing or failing. It has to do with experiencing new ideas and opportunities. If a child discovers a tree at age three for the first time, do they fail if they don't have a name for it, or if they don't understand that it is a coniferous fir tree, or deciduous like a maple? T.S. Eliot asked, "Where is the wisdom we have lost in knowledge and where is the knowledge we have lost in information?" Knowledge and information are good, but they are not enough. That is where we stop reasoning and when we think that having the right knowledge and information is all we need. We think that if we just had the right amount of knowledge and information everything would be in balance. However, I have discovered, that just because a person has knowledge and information about children, doesn't mean they have the wisdom to care for them. Abuse crosses all cultural, economic, ethnic and educational backgrounds.

My daughter came through the front door crying. Her failure was written over her face. Unable to look at me she handed me her test. Trying to talk between sobs and tears, she said, "I failed; I'm near the bottom of the class." I reminded her that in school I was a part of the bottom 10% that made the top 10% percent possible. If it wasn't for me the top ten percent would have no way of knowing they were the top ten percent.

I reminded her of what I had learned many years ago; there are no failures, only lessons. I asked her, "What did you learn?"

"I learned that this subject is not my strong suit. I thought I had to take it because I was told that I needed it to graduate. But I could have taken an equivalent course as a credit that I might have liked better. I needed it just for school. I guess I also know that if I had really wanted to I could have passed. I didn't like the class or the teacher. I didn't do enough of the work to pass."

I asked, "What happened as a result?"

She said, "Now, I'll have to take summer school. I should have listened to you when you encouraged me to take a course that would have better suited my abilities."

"Why did you take the course in the first place?"

"I took it because all my other classmates were telling me I would never amount to anything unless I took this course. I believed them when they said I will never get anywhere in university without having it. I knew they were wrong, but I felt I had to do what they said or they would look down on me and think I am nothing but a failure."

I asked her, "What then was the final lesson?"

"Listen to my heart and not other people."

"Then my dear," I said, "you get an A. You passed the course – Life 101."

Are there no failures, only lessons? Every newborn learns to walk by swimming forward, rolling over, crawling, standing up, tottering along and falling down. They stand, fall; stand, fall. Take a step then fall; take another step and fall again. It is repeated incessantly until they have achieved their goal and are able to move on two legs. They learn by making mistakes and not accepting defeat. They do not begin life walking. They do not view themselves a failure if they don't get it the first time. They do it over and over again until they get it right. They begin by being unable to do anything but eat, sleep and fill their diapers. They don't have to learn how to do these things as they are a natural body function. Everything else they have to learn through trial and error. However, we live in a society that dislikes mistakes and turns its back on the failures that they say make them.

I was never good in school due to being considered, tested, labelled and called "developmentally delayed." I was what people back then called "slow." Yet, today I hold four earned college and university degrees. The last degree was a doctorate. How could that be? I was told by those who "knew," that I would never go to university let alone be successful. My parents were urged to put me in a trade school. I was told I would never amount to much of anything as an adult. I was told that because I couldn't pass English Lit. or math I wouldn't pass through the doors of a university. They were wrong.

I still remember the day the vice-principal came to my grade four class and gave us all the IQ test. I didn't do well. I knew I wouldn't do well. I knew I would never be the smartest. Yet, I knew I could be the fastest. So, I filled in the answers without reading the questions. I finished first. I thought to myself as I handed it in to the vice-principal, "I may not be the smartest, but

I am the fastest." I was pleased with myself. The vice-principal was not. He glared at me, then said aloud, "Class, I want everyone to put down their pencils. I want to introduce you to the dumbest person in your class. He may even be the dumbest person in the world. He is so stupid, he will never amount to anything. This test proves that he is the dumbest person in the world." He raised the test to emphasis his point. He then said, "You can all now go back to doing your test." I was shattered. I went back to my desk and fell apart crying.

I don't remember much after that except telling my parents what happened. I was so ashamed; I knew I had done something wrong and deserved what had happened to me. However, my parents were not angry with me. I remember staying home the next day from school. My father stayed home from work as did my mother. They got a sitter for me and went to the school together. I was somewhat confused by the fact that, though my father had retired from the military the year before after serving for 28 years and fighting in World War II, that morning, he put on his old army uniform as if he were going off to war. I understand now, in a sense he was. I was told a few years later that my father blew past the secretary, went into the vice-principal's office, picked him up and held him against the wall with one arm. I can only guess what he said, but I'm sure it wasn't kind. That ended my journey within the public school educational system. I was given the year and began the following year in the Catholic school system.

Federick Moffett of the Bureau of Instructional Supervision, New York Department of Education wrote "How a Child Learns."

Thus a child learns, by wiggling skills through his fingers and his toes, into himself. By soaking up habits and attitudes of those around him, by pushing and pulling his own world. Thus a child learns, more through trial than error, more through pleasure than pain, more through experience than suggestion and telling, more through suggestion than direction. And thus a child learns through affection, through love, through patience, through understanding, through belonging, through doing and through being. Day by day the child comes to know a little bit of what you know, a little bit more of what you think and understand. That which you dream and believe are in truth what is becoming that child. As you perceive dully or clearly, as you think fuzzily or sharply, as you believe foolishly or wisely, as you dream drably, or goldenly, as you bear false witness or tell the truth, thus a child learns.

Life is not a matter of pass or fail. Life is about learning or not learning, becoming or dying, enjoying or enduring, loving or losing that love. We need to show, tell and teach that this is what it is all about.

Children remind me of what I learned many years ago, that life and learning has nothing to do with passing or failing. The amazing thing about life is that if you don't learn one of the lessons that you need to learn in life, it will come back over and over again until you learn it. That is the reason that the degree that I am most indebted to is the degree I earned from the University of HK, a degree more valuable than all the others. It is even more valuable than the doctorate I worked so hard to achieve. Even today, I continue to return from the lessons I learned at the UHK and the notes I took there to refresh my memory. UHK is the University of Hard Knocks. It taught me and continues to teach me much of what I need to know about achieving a happy and successful life. The fact is, however, many people fail to heed the lessons learned at this university without lecture rooms or campus. They choose to accept only the knowledge or opinions of those in the know who believe there is only one right answer or right way of doing things and that mistakes are wrong and should be avoided at all cost if life's goals are to be achieved.

There were many lessons I learned in the University of Hard Knocks. I learned that if I only listened to what others say, I would get nowhere. I learned that if there is a will there is a way. I learned not to be afraid of failure, in fact I learned to embrace it. I embraced my mistakes, as just one more step along the way.

Babe Ruth struck out more times then he hit home runs. Yet, he isn't remembered for the strike-outs but for the number of times he circled the bases at a jog trot rather than walking back to the dugout from the batter's position at home plate. He is remembered as the home run king not the strike-out king. I learned that life has nothing to do with passing or failing.

I remembered in school that all the children were so afraid of getting a question wrong that they would hide their face in a book, praying they wouldn't be picked to give an answer. At first, I did that too. Later, I discovered that I was wrong so many times, that it began not to matter to me if I got the question wrong. I started making up outlandish answers to the questions being asked. I stretched my mind. As well, I would distract the teacher. Rather than answering his or her question, I would distract them by asking my own questions. I learned more interesting things this way, things I would never have had a chance to learn at that time. The other kids just spouted back the answer the teacher expected, never going beyond the boundaries into the unknown. How could they learn as much as I did using this passive style of becoming educated? Of course, that is because the teacher was considered the authority. They accepted the teacher's authority as being right all the time and their being wrong. I just didn't buy into it.

Years later, this came to a head when a professor in the Masters Degree program said to me, "John, why are you disagreeing with me. I am the professor. I know what is right." As if by being the professor he possessed some God-like knowledge.

"Just because you say it, doesn't make you right. The fact is, I believe you're wrong. You may in fact be right. However, you are going to have to prove it. Just because you say it, doesn't mean I have to accept it." He was so in shock that he sat there with his chin in his hands. I thanked him and left.

I have discovered while studying the lives of the great leaders, artists, scientists, business people that very often they would proceed against conventional wisdom. They'd be willing to make mistakes because they viewed inaccuracies as steps of learning along the way. Failures were seen as lessons. Walt Disney was fired by his editor at a newspaper where he worked for having no good ideas. Disney! What would have happened if he had believed what others had said and given up on his dreams and ideas as a result? We would not have the opportunity to have our children experience the joy of fantasies that have come alive. And we as adults would not have the opportunity to become like little children again.

There are no failures, only lessons. I came to fully realize this by watching my own children and many hundreds of others overcome small and great obstacles alike, through trial and error. As I watched these little children begin to grow, develop, and explore, I found five steps they use to overcome the many obstacles in their lives.

• *Observation*

A child learns first through observation. A baby will observe other children and adults walking and talking. As a result, they begin to learn by watching then talking. They will attempt to do what they saw. They will fall, but because they see it being done, they will continue to attempt to do it until they do it themselves.

• *Action*

The next step is that of taking action. This means making mistakes, and mistakes mean initiative. We see this whenever a child attempts to try something new, whether it is walking, talking, or riding a bike. When they are young, there is no fear of failure. The only fear a child has is that of loud noise and falling. All the other fears they learn from adults. As a result the child is free to attempt things without the belief or apprehension they can't do it. If children feared trying anything new, they would never learn to roll over, then crawl, and then walk as they undertake each step. They repeat their actions over and over. Through trial and error they eventually complete what they are attempting.

• *Confrontation*

Every child confronts and questions conventional wisdom. If the child is very young, they may challenge the conventional wisdom or opinions of doctors and others simply by defying the odds. Not knowing or comprehending that they are unable to do it, they simply confront the obstacle and overcome it.

Baby Sarah came to us from the hospital. The parents abandoned her at birth and said, let the child die. Sarah was less than a pound and was not expected to live. We were told that she would be brain damaged and would likely never be able to walk or talk or respond because she would have Cerebral Palsy. We were asked if we would be willing to go to the hospital to hold and feed her until she died. We said we would. However, we believed and hoped that she would live and come home. Every morning and evening Liane would go and hold, cuddle, kiss and feed her. Each evening I was able, I would before I came home, do the same. After we had helped the children with their homework, and put the little ones to bed, Liane and either Sarah or Alyssa would go back to the hospital to do it all over again. The nurses and doctors were amazed as a month later, at three and half pounds she came home with us. We were still told that the CP was going to be severe. However, we hoped that with physiotherapy, treatment, stimulation and love she would overcome the obstacles. And she did. Soon she was growing, and getting into everything.

• *Correction*

The child makes corrections along the way. As they try, and mistakes are made, they learn from each mistake what adjustments they need to make. With each adjustment they get closer and closer to their goal of walking or speaking or whatever else they are trying to accomplish.

• *Precision*

After the corrections and adjustments are made they continue to do what they have accomplished over and over again until it is done without thought. That is when they have achieved a level of precision.

If children had the conscious awareness of the fear of failure at an early age they would never learn to walk or talk or to do anything for that matter. Perhaps, if we could re-instill in them later in life the fearlessness they had in early childhood, they would not give up on themselves so easily – or us on ourselves.

You can be anything you want to be

"Most people think only once or twice a year.
I have made myself an international reputation by
thinking once or twice a week"
~ George Bernard Shaw

At birth the greatest gift of all is given to almost everyone – life. At birth we are offered this amazing world as a present in which to live and to become anything we want to be. However, as Thoreau realized at Walden Pond, some people go through life and approach death without ever living at all. They never become who they were meant to be. They die before they are really fully born.

Elie Wiesel tells us of a rabbi who said that when we cease to live and meet our Creator, we will not be asked why we did not become a famous person, leader, liberator or to answer the great mysteries of life. The question will simply be – why did you not become you? Why did you not become the fully realized and developed person only you could become?

Through my work with children in our emergency home, with people in my parish, counselling work and my daily life I have discovered that most people are not at all happy. What saddens me is that they don't expect to be happy. They lack self-respect and respect for others because they lack this essential attribute in themselves.

Mental health continues to show a frightening increase of patients in the hospital wards for the mentally ill. There are hundreds of thousands of people who are chronically depressed and in need of treatment, which is often only offered at points of crises and not before. It is believed that one out of every seven people will require some psychological treatment prior to middle age. There are tens of thousands of mentally and emotionally disturbed children between the ages of 5 to 19.

Child abuse is at epidemic proportions. And it may well soon become one of the prime causes of childhood hospitalization. It has become common in our work to see children so beaten that they have become brain damaged or blinded, being tortured and burned with cigarettes and scalded with boiling water or who are totally repressed due to parent abuse.

Though I should, by this time, no longer be surprised or shocked, I am filled with despair every time. It continues to stun and bewilder me that given the choice between joy and sorrow, delight or despair, most people will choose sorrow and despair every time. Rather than being and becoming all they could be, people invariably choose apathy, anger, violence, anything to live in a personal anguish.

Every year people come to the United States and Canada for a better life. But they bring their emotional and psychological baggage with them, which hinders them from achieving a proper place in our promised land.

We received yet another call late one night. We were asked to receive a baby along with his eight-year-old brother. The worker was aware that we were open for infants to five-year-olds but went on to explain the situation.

The brothers were coming from a murder. They didn't want to separate them due to the circumstances. The person that was murdered was their brother. He was six. His stepmother had killed him while the father watched television downstairs. Later, it was discovered that the father had in the past also been involved in abusing the boys. The older brother ran to his father for help while the murder was being committed. He was told by his father not to bother him. That night, as his brother lay dying in his arms, the oldest boy tried to wash the blood and vomit off his younger brother in a bath and comfort him as best he could, while trying to feed his baby brother as well.

He carried him into his bed and held him all night long. He awoke in the morning to discover his brother beside him, dead. His father called 911 and throughout the day the police and workers tried to piece together what happened. It was late that night when they finally allowed the children to leave the house with the CAS worker.

There was never a question in our minds as to whether or not we would receive them. We did. The worker gave us the details that we needed. She told us that the eight-year-old and his baby brother were stepbrothers. The eight-year-old and his dead brother were born in Jamaica. Their mother still lives there. The baby was their half-brother.

The eight-year-old came through the door clutching his baby brother. He was still covered in the blood and vomit from his dead sibling. They had not been able to get him to put his baby brother down. He watched us intently. He searched out whether or not this would be a place of safety. He scrutinized every interaction we had with the workers, the police and our own children to see how we would respond. He was examining carefully everything we did. He was in shock. He was terrified. Yet, he was very protective of his baby brother.

Eventually his defenses began to come down long enough for us to feed, change and clothe his brother. We encouraged him to have a bath and change into clean pajamas. We assured him that he could sleep in the same room as his brother and that he could be with him as long as we took care of him. Due to the media attention the children were well protected from having to be returned to the parents who abused them, and killed their brother. Justice was swift. The parents were charged and convicted. Sadly, the brothers were separated because they had different mothers. The baby was adopted, and the older brother was returned to his birth mother in Jamaica.

Why do people persist in making choices that destroy their lives and the lives of others? Orim Meikle, a black minister in Toronto graphically addressed the issue of violence within the black community at the funeral of a black youth murdered by another black youth. "Our children carry guns like we used to carry bubblegum," he told the mourners. "Our children are made to feel and to believe that to be tough, especially in our black culture, somehow creates manhood and virility within you." He ended with, "Most of our children spend half their lives in jail."

Betsy Powell, the crime reporter for the *Toronto Star* stated that Orim Meikle blamed parents for not setting rules and said, "We're not working together as a community to eradicate violence. Things have got to change...we're going to kill ourselves, we're committing genocide in our culture." He added that for change to come, fathers need to return to the home, doing away with absentee fathers who breed children like racehorses – people are not racehorses.

Violence begets violence. If there is violence in the home, it is inevitable that the violence will extend outside the home. The disrespect we have for others is actually a complete disrespect for ourselves! That, however, doesn't have to be the case. We have the power to make better choices. We have the right to have a better life. Is Elie Wiesel right? Is the only question everyone must ask is, "Why we are not becoming who only we can become?" If it is, why aren't we?

I have learned from my many little children that you can be and do anything you want if you really want it.

While driving my fifteen-year-old daughter to school she asked me with a tone of desperation in her voice, "Daddy, what do you think I should be when I grow up? After all, I'm in grade 10 and there is not much time left. I have to know what I want to be – and I don't!"

"Darling," I said, "you have all the time you need to do what you want. Let me tell you something. You can be, do and have anything you want. If you really want it."

Frustrated she said, "I knew you were going to say that. That's of no help at all."

She went on to give a litany of things she learned that she couldn't do in school and reasons why she would not be able to be in a certain profession because of it. To which I said, "If you *really* want to be, do or have something, you will. It is as easy as learning the ABCs." I reminded her that there was a time in my life people told me I would never be able to go to University. They told me that my marks were not good enough. Yet, I believed in the old adage, "If there is a will there is a way." I knew I had the will to complete a university degree even if others thought I couldn't. I just had to find the way to do it. I reminded her that not only did I get one university degree but four. The last degree was a doctorate. "Remember," I said, "you can be, do and have anything you want if you truly want it. It is as simple as the ABCs."

I also reminded her of little baby Cynthia. Cynthia was born weighing less then a pound. After giving birth to what the doctor's called a micro-preemie, the mother was told that Cynthia would likely be severely disabled and demand a great deal of care if she lived at all. In response the mother said sourly, "Let her die." After which her mother disappeared into the night.

I reminded my daughter that we were called by the workers and doctors to care for this tiny child. "You remember don't you," I said, "how you went down to the hospital with your mother and me, and held her and loved her and fed her? Don't you remember how small she was? She was able to fit into the palm of my hand. You remember, don't you, how the doctor said she may not live and if she did, she would have to have a great deal of care and attention?" She nodded. "You remember how many late nights and early mornings we had at the hospital feeding her until that great day when she came home to us weighing three pounds. You remember all the obstacles, she had to overcome. You remember all the doctor's appointments, physiotherapy and specialist appointments she needed after she came home to us. Just think of all she had to overcome. And you remember how happy we all were when the doctor told us that she was going to be just fine." At this she began to weep because she also remembered that it was not long after that, that this sweet little child was adopted and left us to begin her new life in another loving home. I gently told her, "Darling, you did that for her. We did that for her. If you can do that, you can do anything."

Life is filled with obstacles. We can use them or be used up by them. We can overcome them, or be overcome by them. It is up to us.

"My life is filled with many obstacles," said Jack Parr. "The greatest obstacle is me."

The ABCs of Life

The number one principle of success was declared by Napoleon Hill when he stated: "Whatever your mind can Conceive, and you choose to Believe, you will most certainly Achieve." This is the ABC's, or the CBA's of success. It might seem too simple to be beneficial, but it is not. Contained within this statement is the power to make anything happen. Every child instinctively knows and lives out this principle of success until they are taught to give up on it and themselves.

No one told Cynthia that she couldn't live, grow, crawl, stand and then walk. She did those very things in spite of the obstacles and what others said. When she was given the opportunity, the encouragement, the food, the nurturing, love, and the therapy that was needed she accomplished what she wanted. She was too young to be influenced negatively by outside opinions. Her little body did what her mind told it to do. On a very immature level she and her natural instinct *conceived* in her mind what she wanted to do. She *believed* in spirit that she could crawl, and then walk and she, like all other babies, learned how to do it by trial and error.

Too often, we allow ourselves to be hindered in achieving a fulfilling life and doing what we truly want because we believe that the obstacles are too great. We believe the negative opinions of others, instead of believing in ourselves.

Cynthia overcame and continues to overcome great obstacles because she was believed in, and she believed that she could. The challenge in the future will be the same for her as it is for all of us. The challenge will be to continue to believe in herself and not in the obstacles or the negative opinions of others.

Many years ago, someone conceived the idea that there must be something better and more comfortable to sit on than a rock or the ground. The conception spurred that person into action. They thought of something they called a "chair." And ever since that time, that thought has allowed us to sit comfortably on many variations of that simple concept of a chair. Thoughts are things. Whatever your mind can conceive and you believe, you will achieve. You can be, do and have anything you want in life if you truly want it. A little child learns to walk and talk because they saw it being done and thought on some infantile level, "I want to do that." The result is that despite the obstacles it gets done. And not only that, they can learn any language on earth.

This means a simple change in thinking can change your life.

Most of us don't think too much about what we are thinking. Nor do we think about the way we think. By changing the way we are thinking we can change the course of our lives.

We must start *thinking* for a change; and we must start thinking for a *change*. Did you notice that simply by changing the emphasis on one or another word in the statement, it changes the meaning of the statement? This is what I mean by changing our thinking. If someone said to you, "You must start *thinking* for a change," you might consider that statement an insult. You might consider that the person is saying that you are stupid; or that you don't think very much. If however, someone were to say, "You must start thinking for a *change*," you might consider this statement a challenge. It seems to suggest that if you want to change your life situation, you must change the way you are thinking. There is a silent challenge within the statement. It seems to say, "You must start thinking for a *change to occur.*"

When we challenge our thinking we change our thinking.

No one ought to think of themselves as someone who is unable to achieve success in life. Helen Keller had hundreds of roadblocks and obstacles that interfered with her success. Yet, with the help of Anne Sullivan she learned to overcome what seemed to be the insurmountable obstacle of her blindness and become a writer and painter and advocate for the blind. Could you think of a higher calling to challenge a blind person than to paint? She had the insight to not allow her obstacles to hinder her from believing that anything is possible.

Too often we dismiss the thought, idea, and creative impulse that we have out of hand because we have a preconceived judgment that states that it is not realistic. It is at this point we must stop and rethink that preconception. Just because it may have been true for you in the past does not mean that it is right for you now. You are not the person you were last year, or last month, or last week or even in the last few minutes. You have been changed and are being changed by everything around you. Hopefully by what you are reading.

Heraclitus stated, "You can not step into the same stream twice." It's true. The stream is continually changing. And the stepping in changes it. And the stepping out changes it. Change is the one constant. So be specific; you can't step into the same water once.

Business Week magazine reported that a child of five is vastly more creative than an adult of 40. An adult is only two percent as creative as a child of that age. Why do we allow barriers to be put in the way of our creativity, causing us to fail to achieve the success and happiness that is our right from an early age? From a young age, children are taught to conform to a certain set of behaviours and attitudes about themselves, their world, and their place in it. They allow these forces, often urged on by parents and siblings, to make them conform to certain social, educational, intellectual and societal standards. As a result it becomes increasingly more difficult to keep thinking creatively. How sad that they dismiss out of hand the imaginative and creative thoughts that would bring about a passionately fulfilling and prosperous life to them later.

In a marvelous book called, *The World of Children*, Anthony Storr says it would be good if all the adults in the world could get back in touch with what it was like at the beginning of their process as children. Every one of us goes through the process of finding our first flower or tree and experiencing the marvel and magic of it all. However, every one of us also goes through the indignity of having no control over anything. Yet, fearlessly we venture on until we are brought to a halt because we are told we are not allowed to do what we saw could be done.

Being a child can be humiliating. Storr stated, "To be so small that you can be picked up, to be moved about at the whim of others. To be fed or not to be fed. To be cleaned or to be left dirty, made happy or left to cry. It's surely so ultimate an indignity that it's not surprising that some of us never really recover from it. For it is surely one of the basic fears of human kind that we should be treated as things and not as persons. Manipulated, pushed around by impersonal forces, we are treated as of no account by the powerful and more superior. Each one is a tiny atom in an enormous human universe, but we need the illusion that we count – that our individuality demands attention. To be able to be totally disregarded as a person is a kind of death in life against which we are compelled to fight with all our strength."

I have discovered that it is the person who still contains within them that child with its optimism and adventure that achieves their dreams in this world. It is the non-conformists that achieve greatness. Leaders, philosophers and others who wish to make a difference in their lives and the world, have to be willing to change their views and pre-conditioned perceptions of reality about themselves, and their world if they are going to achieve success. Look at the many great leaders – Abraham Lincoln, Martin Luther King, Jr., Mother Teresa, Bishop Tutu, Nelson Mandela, Maya Angelou, Oprah Winfrey. I am sure you could name many others. If any one of these men or women had gone along with the world or the status quo, think of where we would be today. Ralph Waldo Emerson drew this conclusion, "What lies behind us and what lies before us are tiny matters compared to what lies within us."

If you are to achieve your dreams and accomplish the seemingly impossible; you must make the choice to dismiss the need to conform to those set behaviours that are negative and life-negating. You must be willing to forgo the approval of others; and accept your own opinion of yourself and your dreams as being right and achievable – and become like a child again.

Having done this, you then must trust your own creativity and ingenuity. You must pay attention to your thought – for thoughts are things. You must pay attention to your dreams – because dreams do come true. You must pay attention to your true self – for you are a child of God.

We are so afraid to be who and what we are. We get amazing magical and insane ideas and we don't act on them. You see your child and think, "I could just hug her, hug her and hug her and tell her, 'I love you so much it hurts. I'm so proud of you!'" But the thought passes and back you go to your work. And she and you lose out on an awesome experience, just because you think, "She already knows. I don't need to tell her." For God's sake tell her! Even if she thinks you're crazy.

I did this to my daughter Alyssa. She looked at me in horror, and said, "What's going on? Are you doing to die or something?!"

I said, "Only, if I don't tell you I love you."

She paused, then hugged me, and said, "I love you too, Daddy." So she thinks I'm crazy. She's not the first.

There is a chapter in *Wind, Sand and Stars* that is beautiful. It speaks of love as I have never heard it spoken of before. Saint Exupéry says, "Perhaps love is the process of my leading you gently back to yourself." It is not my trying to make you in my image or in the image of another, but leading you gently back to your true self. That more than anything else is what we have tried lovingly, desperately, and haltingly to do in our life and in the lives of those we come in touch with.

If you stand for nothing, you will fall for anything

Life is not lost by dying; life is lost minute by minute, day by dragging day, in all the thousand small uncaring ways.
~ Stephen Vincent Benet

Liane and I both felt we needed a break after 15 years of intense work with children. After she had taken a trip with her mother and I cared for the children, I went on a retreat to a monastery.

During the seven day retreat each participant would have a private interview with one of the monks to ensure things were going well. It was a guided silent retreat. No one was allowed to have contact with anyone. There was no communication, and no eye contact. The only contact was with your spiritual advisor once each day for a half hour. At one point about five days in, I began to question everything I believed. I thought I was going to go nuts. All the silence was getting to me. When you are used to having the noise of at least seven children all around, as I have, the silence can be deafening.

I told the monk at the interview that I thought I was losing it, saying that everything I ever believed in at that moment didn't seem to make any sense. "I don't know what is true anymore."

I thought that he would give me my much needed comfort and assurance, but he didn't. He spoke one word, "Good."

"What do you mean good? How can that be good?"

He said, "It's good, because most of what you believe isn't true anyway. You must empty yourself of all that you have previously believed about what is and isn't true and right. Having done this, you will begin to see whatever is actually true, noble, honourable, pure, lovely, and excellent. Having discovered that, you can think on those things. And once you have accomplished that, you can live from there."

I was stunned into silence, knowing he was right. Much of what we comprehend in life as the big things that we stand for, or are driven to acquire, are neither true, honourable, noble, lovely, pure or excellent. And that which is true and honourable, etc., will remain that no matter what, and these must then become the guiding principles of life if we are to have a meaningful and fulfilling life that stands for something.

What do you stand for? What are the values, morals, or standards that are the guiding principles in your life? We all have them. We may not all agree on what they are or use them the same way; however, we all have them. For some the guiding principle may simply be following the golden rule; "Do unto others as you would have them do unto you." For others it may be the Ten Commandments. For still others it may be to love God and their neighbour as themselves.

One of the guiding principles or values in my life that came back to me at the retreat was from a prophet called Micah. He said, "He has told you, O people, what is good; and what does the Lord require of you but to do justice, to love mercy, and to walk humbly with your God?"[1]

I have found this little phrase intensely helpful when dealing with the difficult challenges that we have to face in life. We are to do justly, love mercy and walk humbly with God. It is so very simple, yet so profound.

Live Justly

One of the most profound statements from Elie Wiesel is, "There may be times when we are powerless to prevent injustice, but there must never be a time when we fail to protest."

Many years ago when Liane and I came face to face with the violence being done to children in our country and city, we knew that we must do something. Justice demanded it. Mercy required it, and God called for it.

There was never a question in our minds as to whether or not we would care for these hundreds of children. I say to myself and others, "If you stand for nothing, then you will fall for anything." It was, therefore, never a question of *if* we would do it, but *how*. Part of the answer was to simply open our home to these little ones. And nearly 1000 infants and young children have entered our hearts since the decision. Yet, injustice, poverty, cruelty and brutality against women and children remain. Nearly 20 years have passed since we first began to do this work, first in child protection and the treatment of emotionally disturbed children in Thunder Bay, and later as the primary emergency home for infants and children in Toronto. Yet, the problem persists and grows.

I was approached after I said this at a speaking engagement by a man who said, "It sounds to me that you are fighting a losing battle. You might as well just give up. You aren't making a difference. After all, things are getting worse not better." I told him that I understood his frustration because it was my own. I then introduced him to my beautiful daughter. He knew immediately his argument was lost. For standing before him was a bright, beautiful, and delightful Jamaican-Canadian seven-year-old whom we love deeply and whom we adopted after she came to us due to very difficult circumstances.

We may not be able to change the whole world for a child, but we can change a child's whole world. We have made it our mission in life to change each child's world that we come in contact with; even if that contact is to share but a brief encounter with them.

A just society is simply a gathering of people who wish to live justly; especially with the most vulnerable in our community. The problem is that within every society there are people who choose to rampage through lives of brutality, stupidity and cruelty, without conscience or the concern for the consequences. It is for that reason that it is all the more important for us who say that we want a society that is just, loving, merciful and compassionate, to choose to live that way ourselves.

Love Mercy

A recent article in *The Readers' Digest* written by Claire Safran was a deeply moving story about seventy-nine-year-old Clara Hale and the drug-addicted infants she cares for in her home in Harlem. In an old bentwood rocker, she soothes a hurting child. I read the story eagerly because it reminded me of our own work.

"I love you and God loves you," she promises. "Your mother loves you too, but she's sick right now, like you are." She coaxes the baby to nurse at a bottle. She bathes the child, croons softly, tries a little patty-cake game.

"After a while, maybe you get a smile," she tells a visitor. "So you know the baby's trying too. You keep loving the child – and you wait."

The title of this moving story is *Mama Hale and Her Little Angels*. It tells of Clara Hale, who has spent a lifetime caring for other women's children. In a fifth-floor walkup, she raised forty foster children as well as three of her own. And now she operates a place called Hale House, a unique haven in the heart of the drug darkness of New York. At the time the article was written, she had cared for 487 babies of addicts. Since then, there have been many more.

Mama Hale says, "The ones who worry [me] most are the toddlers who arrive scruffy and neglected." The article about her goes on, "Against the disorder of the world they will return to someday, she teaches them a sense of order – regular meals and bedtimes. A clean house and clothes." "They don't always know what I am saying," she says, "but they know I love them." That is part of her gift, as she calls it, her secret for saving children and saving their lives.

It doesn't take much to change the world. It just takes the willingness to do what you know you can do.

A very interesting incident took place at the University of California at Berkeley. Maintenance men went into a storage room and found a stack of university printed pamphlets called *Control of Termites*. But they discovered that the entire stack of pamphlets had been eaten through by termites. Obviously the university knew how to solve the problem of termites, but didn't act on the knowledge they had.

We too have the knowledge on what to do. The question remains, "Do we have the wisdom to use it?" It doesn't matter where we start. It only matters that we do something. It doesn't matter if the issue that impassions you is the environment, recycling, violence against women, child poverty, peace, ecology, or education. It only matters that you stand for something.

"The only thing that allows evil to flourish is that good people do nothing." Every one of us *can and must* do something.

In New Orleans, Louisiana, there was an oil millionaire who wanted to do something to make a difference in the lives of children. He adopted an inner-city school that had a dropout rate of 84%. Only 16 percent of the school in any given year would graduate. That means in a class of 25 kids only 2 would graduate. He told the students that if they graduated from high school, with good grades, and attended school 95 percent of the time he would pay for their entire university fees.

He took the children to the university, paired them with a university student who took them to class, the campus, and the cafeteria. He had them see just what would happen if they only believed. He asked the teachers to take a few moments every morning to remind the students what they would be working toward and holding out the promise of a better life. When the children finally graduated, the dropout rate fell from 84 percent to less than 20 percent. Now, rather than only two graduating and 23 dropping out, 23 graduated and only two dropped out![2]

One person made the difference.

You may be saying, I am no millionaire; I could never do that. That may be true, but don't be negative about what you *can* do.

I read an amazing story about a boy by the name of Tommy Tighe. "He was six years old at the time. He had what he thought was a great idea. The idea was to create bumper stickers that said, "PEACE, PLEASE! DO IT FOR US KIDS, signed Tommy Tighe." He borrowed the $454.00 dollars so that he could print the bumper stickers. He began by selling them to everyone he knew. They began popping up on cars everywhere and people were calling his home to get more.

Tommy had convinced his father to drive him to Ronald Reagan's home. Tommy rang the bell and the gatekeeper came out. He told the gatekeeper what he wanted to do. He sold one to the gatekeeper. The gatekeeper then said to wait a minute and got the former President. After he achieved that he sent one to Mikhail Gorbachev with a bill for $1.50. Gorbachev sent back the $1.50.

Tommy's project took off and he got written up in the newspapers and went on the news and talk shows. While on Joan Rivers' show he wowed Joan and the crew and the whole audience. All of them pulled out their wallets and bought the sticker. At the end of the show, Joan leaned in and said, "Tommy, do you really think your bumper sticker will cause peace in the world?"

Tommy said, "Well, So far I've had it out for less than two

years and I already got the Berlin Wall down. I'm doing pretty good, don't you think?"[3]

I hold on to true stories like these because they remind me that everyone who is willing to do what they can with what they have can make an increasing difference in our world.

Walk Humbly

I live a blessed life. I was again reminded of this when we brought two children to the clinic. They had arrived at our home at 12:30 a.m. They had been in and out of care all their lives. They were two and a half and four years old. A neighbour had called the police. They were found hanging over the balcony of their twelfth floor apartment. Their mother was passed out on the couch, drunk or high. The police didn't wait to find out. They left a note to tell her that she could contact the Children's Aid Society for her children. The worker told us after arriving that they had just closed the file on this family, releasing them back to the mother. She had been sober and clean just long enough to get her kids and a welfare cheque to pay for their keep, but it is obvious where it went.

"There But By the Grace of God …!"

Liane sat down to wait for the doctor from Children's Aid to examine them. Sitting beside her was a young girl. Liane commented on how beautiful she was. She was bi-racial. She reminded Liane of our seven-year-old daughter Tabitha. She looked to be 14 years old. After she went into the examination room to meet with the doctor, Liane asked about her. Liane asked how she was doing, and if she had been "in care" for long. The worker said she was just picked up again. She had been in and out of care for most of her life. At this point she was two months pregnant, and was arrested for prostitution, and drug possession.

Liane stared at her in shocked silence. She was thinking, "That could have been Tabitha."

"There but by the grace of God..."

If only we had a mansion so we could just open our door to these children, and a "Hummer" to transport them to all their visits, appointments with workers and doctors. If only we could just gather them in our arms and tell them that they are loved and they don't have to allow themselves to be used and abused and do drugs to kill the pain of the loss and emptiness. For now, we must simply live justly, love mercy and walk humbly with God; while recognizing that "There but by the grace of God go I."

[1] Bible: Micah
[2] Jack Canfield and Mark Victor Hansen, *The Aladdin Factor*, Berkley Book, New York, New York, 1995, pg. 93
[3] Jack Canfield and Mark Victor Hansen, *The Aladdin Factor*, Berkley Book, New York, New York, 1995, pp. 52, 53

You can make a difference

The final lesson I learned through caring for children is that you can make a difference just by the way you live your life. The life you live impacts the people around you and leaves a lasting legacy for good or ill. The most profound impact will be felt by your family.

Jennifer arrived on one Friday evening at 11:30 p.m. She was three months old. Her mother was thirteen. Her grandmother was twenty-seven and her great-grandmother was in her early forties. We didn't ask about her great-great-grandmother. From what the worker could tell us, each of them had been involved with Children's Aid. Their family file was thick, and their legacy spanned the generations. Jennifer left us a few days later to be raised in the care of Children's Aid, as her mother went out to "party" before going into the clinic for her second abortion. This was not a cycle of success. It was a cycle of loss and pain and loneliness. That is why intervention, prevention, and protection must take place to break these types of cycles.

What we believe, how we think, and how we live our lives influence others for better or worse. I came to understand the truth of this when I heard of the life legacy of Jonathan Edwards and Max Jukes who had lived vastly different lives. However, both impacted the lives of their family and community for generations.

Benjamin B. Warfield, who was perhaps one of the most

famous professors in the history of Princeton University, researched the life of Jonathan Edwards and Max Jukes. He analyzed 1,394 descendants of Jonathan Edwards and 1,200 descendants of Max Jukes.

Jonathan Edwards, who had been perhaps the greatest philosopher-theologian the world has ever known, became president of Princeton University in 1758.

Warfield discovered that of the over thirteen hundred descendants of Edwards,

- 13 became college presidents
- 65 became college professors
- 30 became judges
- 100 became lawyers
- 60 became physicians
- 3 became United States senators
- 80 became public servants in various capacities

Warfield found in contrast that Max Jukes, who had been an atheist and criminal, had

- 300 descendants who died as paupers
- 150 who were criminals (including 7 murderers)
- 100 who were alcoholics
- 50% of the female descendants became prostitutes
- 540 cost the state $1.25 million[1]

The descendants of Edwards were not the only ones who were the beneficiaries of the legacy of Edwards. Timothy Dwight, one of the grandsons of Edwards, became President of Yale University. One of his students was Lyman Beecher. Beecher became the President of Lane Seminary in Ohio. His daughter Harriet Beecher Stowe became a famous author and wrote *Uncle Tom's Cabin*. His daughter Catharine founded the Western Female Institute which later became Miami University in Oxford, Ohio.

Beecher's son, Henry Ward Beecher, became the most influential writer, thinker and speaker of his time and served at Brooklyn's Plymouth Church. His son, Edward, became the first President of Illinois College, and his daughter Isabella Beecher Hooker was very involved in organizing the cause of women's rights to vote.[2] Every one of these people was the beneficiary of the Edward's legacy. He made a difference in the lives of hundreds of people without even knowing it.

You might say, "I am no Jonathan Edwards and I am certainly no Max Jukes. So what can I do?" Let me assure you that you can make a difference by the choices you make and the actions you take, and the gifts and talents you use for the betterment of your family, community and country.

The choices you make and the actions you take are like ripples in a pond, each ripple extending further and further out. Your actions and decisions have an effect on others.

This truth was made dramatically clear the day when two people became disgusted by the plight of a horribly abused little girl who they helped to be declared an "animal" under the law so that she could be protected by the law preventing cruelty to animals. There was no legal protection for her as a child at that time. The only protection was as an animal. That one act caused a ripple effect that changed the course of history for children.

Children in Crisis: An Historical Context

It was in 1893 – just over 110 years ago – that the Provincial Government of Ontario passed the Child Protection Act. Prior to that, children had no protection except for orphanages.

It was John Joseph Kelso who organized in 1895 the first "Conference on Saving Children" in Canada's history. He was outraged at the plight of the children in Toronto who were being abused and who had to panhandle and engage in prostitution due to their poverty. He modeled and founded the Toronto Humane Society for the prevention of cruelty to children and animals after The Societies for the Prevention of Cruelty to Animals, which was established in 1874 in the United States.[3]

The Societies for the Prevention of Cruelty to Animals had long been in existence and laws were in place to protect livestock and pets in the United States. It was not until a child by the name of Mary Ellen was discovered horribly abused that these laws were ever used to protect children. "The Society" grudgingly brought forward her case with the urging of Etta Wheeler, a "sweet faced missionary," and a newspaper reporter by the name of Jacob Riis. Etta Wheeler understood the power of the press and used it to force "The Society" to spearhead the case. It was at a time of social upheaval. The influence of the women's suffrage movement and the debate over Darwinism became entwined with Mary Ellen's case. That gave it its power. The combined forces of social change caused the courts to declare Mary Ellen an "animal" under the law. The result was that she was protected and the laws were enacted that later created the Societies for the Prevention of Cruelty to Animals and Children.[4] This later gave birth to the Children's Aid Society that we know today.

All this happened because one person – Henry Kelso – decided to make a difference. There have been many changes in child welfare since that time when a child had to be declared an "animal" to be protected under the law. Things are better, but there are moments when I wonder by how much. Animals still, it seems to me, are often better protected by the law than children.

Child Protection Today

Abuse against children is still treated as a domestic problem and not a crime; just as spousal abuse was considered at one time a domestic problem and not a crime. As a result, children who have been dreadfully abused are returned time after time to those who abused them.

We have noticed since we began our work in child welfare twenty years ago, and our fostering fifteen years ago, and our emergency home twelve years ago, that the severity of the abuse is getting gradually worse. The crisis is widening and worsening. Can this be stopped?

At one time, we would receive children who were neglected due to lack of parental ability or addiction to alcohol. These children were returned with various support systems put in place for the child and family. There was perhaps the occasional child who came with bruises or a broken bone. Today that seems to be the norm. There are over 300,000 children in Canada who are in the care and/or supervision of Children's Aid because of abuse and neglect.

There are more children in need of a place of protection than there are homes willing to take them. We need 1200 *new* loving homes in Toronto alone. This number will barely keep our heads above water. At one time there was approximately the same number of homes willing to receive children as there were children to be placed. Today there are more children in need of protection and a place of safety than there are homes to provide that place of protection and safety. The Children's Aid Foundation has created a program called, "Homes for Kids" to try to address this need for stable, loving, extraordinary people who will open their hearts and homes to care for these children.

There is a coming tidal wave of which we are only starting to experience the effects. The dilemma we are facing is that just as we are beginning to deal with this tidal wave of abuse, the most experienced social workers are retiring, the remaining workers are burning out due to the workload, the good foster homes are being stretched to the limit, and the few sub-standard ones may in fact be allowed to remain open because there is no place to put the children. The agencies are being overwhelmed due to the need, the funding is inadequate and there are fears that it will dry up, and the courts are still focusing on protecting and preserving the abusive homes instead of advocating for and protecting the child.

In 1998 there were 135,000 child abuse investigations conducted in Canada with children under the age of sixteen. That is 21.5 investigations per one thousand children. Only 1.75 per one thousand children were removed from their homes and placed in the care of Children's Aid.[5]

Though it is true that in Canada there are child welfare laws that require that all cases of suspected child abuse must be investigated to determine if a child is in need of protection, it is not necessarily true, due to how the courts interpret and implement the law, that they will receive that protection in the long run.

If it is determined, after investigation that a child is in need of protection, the child welfare authorities may respond by either "providing counseling or support for the family, removing the child (temporarily or permanently) from the home, or removing the abuser(s) from the home. Criminal sanctions may also apply in cases of sexual or physical abuse." However, it is not necessarily true that the parents who are proven to have assaulted the child will be charged or jailed for that offence.[6] These procedures must be reformed.

Reforming the Law and Enhancing its Implementation

There is a task force called *The Children as Victims Project* that has been created by the Department of Justice of Canada. The purpose of this project is to review and consult with the various provincial and territorial partners as well as the general public to determine if there is need for further reforms to criminal law and policy specific to children.

The Project is exploring:

- **adding new child-specific offences to the *Criminal Code*.** Child-specific offences under review include: criminal physical abuse of a child, criminal neglect of a child, criminal emotional abuse of a child, child homicide, and failing to report suspected crimes against children.
- **ensuring that the *Criminal Code* provisions concerning age of consent are appropriate.** The areas under review include raising the general age of consent to sexual activity, and a possible amendment to ensure that a child victim's apparent consent cannot be used as a defence.
- **ensuring that the *Criminal Code* contains sentencing provisions to better protect children.** Possible modifications currently under review include provisions to: specifically emphasize the importance of denunciation and deterrence of crimes against children; provide the courts with additional tools to require longer-term supervision and mandate the availability of treatment for offenders who pose a continuing danger of re-offending against children; recognize the frequency and seriousness of child abuse in the home and at the hands of parents and caretakers; encourage the courts, when sentencing offenders in these cases, to place less emphasis on an offender's previous good character, since it is not unusual for such offenders to lack a prior criminal record; and require the courts to emphasize the emotional and psychological harms caused to children in assessing the gravity of the offences and the conduct involved.[7]

Though these reforms look positive, they do not go far enough in recognizing the fact that violence against children is a crime.

The Importance of Prevention

The field of Child Welfare has, out of necessity, concentrated on families-at-risk, rather than focusing on developing and providing preventative measures that increase family wellness. In the environment in which we now live, it means that we must, in Child Welfare, begin to move beyond protection to prevention – while simultaneously dealing with the current and ongoing issues of child protection – if we are ever going to stem the tide of child abuse and maltreatment.

Studies conducted on the few preventative programs already in existence have shown the effectiveness of this course of action and have revealed that children and families can benefit from this type of pre-emptive intervention.[8]

When the necessary support systems are in place prior to the development of stressful life events, and the added stressors of poverty and the lack of adequate and affordable housing are removed, the likelihood of a child becoming "at-risk" is diminished.[9]

Most of the parents who come to the attention of the child welfare agencies have not seriously abused their children. However, the resources expended to investigate and apprehend these children, only to return them a short time later to their abusers, are astronomical.

"A large majority are trying very hard to do well for their children and themselves, often confronting difficulties that most professional helpers cannot truly comprehend. These parents do not benefit from being legally investigated under threat of losing their children if they do not measure up to our expectations. If we want to improve the well-being of children and parents in these families, we need to move toward a positive system of child and family welfare where our first response in most situations is 'How can we help?'"[10]

We must be present in the areas of our country and communities where people need the most help. We must create and implement programs that avert problems before they begin. It is my contention that at least some of the stress and pressure on the Child Welfare system could be diminished if these other measures of intervention and governmentally funded community based programs were created, considered and utilized.

For this to occur, Governments must be willing to address the economic, social, and environmental issues that impact and increase the likelihood of child abuse. The Government must then be willing to adequately fund the programs that address these issues.

Of course, accountability must be built into these funding programs so the children and families reap the benefit. These programs ought to be monitored to show that there is a credible and measurable benefit to those communities and families receiving the intervention.

If we fail or refuse to seriously create and implement preventative measures, our Child Welfare system will be overrun and we will be a civilization overwhelmed by the legacy of the Max Jukes of our society, instead of blessed by those who leave a legacy like Jonathan Edwards

You Too Can Make a Difference

There is something more that can be done. A more immediate and personal way of making a difference is that of becoming a foster parent. There is an immense need for high-quality loving homes for the abused children. CAS needs devoted people who are willing to become foster parents. A person who cares for children is on the front line of humanity, whether they are a mother or father, teacher, or social worker, or caregiver, or guardian, or foster family. That person or family is creating a lasting legacy. They are impacting humanity. They are transforming society. And it all begins with you.

Foster Parent Misconceptions

The fact is that the vast majority of the families that care for abused children do so lovingly and selflessly. They willingly give of their time, energy, talent and compassion to make the life of a child a little better and their future a bit brighter. However, there have been, in the past, sub-standard homes that have not provided the best care for these needy children. The Children's Aid Society ceases the service provided in these homes as soon as they become aware of them. That is why it is so important that loving people who desire to make a difference do so by opening their home to these children.

Secondly, it is generally thought by some taxpayers that the majority of those who are foster parents are in it for the money. There are those, in the past, that make that a partial truth. The standard payment per day for fostering a child is $25.14. That works out to be $1.05 an hour. My daughter makes more money when she baby-sits for three hours for the neighbours. I could think of better ways to make money; but not a better way to make a difference.

The fact is that the majority of those who are foster parents do this work because they care deeply for the welfare of children. To their great credit the facts show that nearly 70% of all the foster parents in the United States and Canada eventually adopt a child, and 50% of those same parents adopt more than one child. If they were in fostering only for the money then they would never adopt. The money stops for the foster parent once the adoption papers are finalized.

Adoption Misconception

Every year, in each agency of the Children's Aid Society, through-out the United States and Canada there are hundreds of children available for adoption. You may be shocked but there are approximately 70,000 children available for adoption in Canada today. In the year 2000, there were approximately 6,000 children in Ontario alone, who were available for adoption and in need of loving people who were willing to adopt them. Only 10% of these children were adopted. This is true for most years. In some of the provinces the percentage of those adopted is as low as four or five percent. Those who were adopted will soon be replaced by others in need of adoption. Another 350 couples go overseas at great expense to adopt children each year rather than adopt locally.[11]

Sandra Martin, in an article in the *National Post* states that the total cost for adoption overseas starts at approximately $20,000 and can go as high as $40,000 to adopt a child. These costs include $900 to $1800 for a home study; $1,750 to $2,500 for the first instalment of Agency fees; $5,000 for travel and accommodations; $5,000 US to $15,000 US for Foreign/program fees; orphanage donations that vary in amount; a second instalment for the Agency of $1,750 to $2,750. There are extra costs that add to the total, including $100 for immigration fees; $250 for post-adoption assessment; and a $925 fee for Ontario residents.[12]

There remains a misconception in the minds of perspective adoptive parents that it takes thousands of dollars to adopt in Canada, that it takes years to complete the procedure to adopt and that there are very few if any children available for adoption in Canada.

The truth is it takes the same length of time as giving birth – approximately nine months. And like giving birth, it is free to adopt through the Children's Aid Society. *There is no cost to the adoptive parent.*

The benefit of adopting locally is that you will be given the birth history of the child. The reality of adopting overseas is that you will not necessarily be given this information, and the infor-

mation that you are given may not be true. There are countless
stories of people who have adopted children from Russia and
other countries, only to find out that these countries had been
dumping their damaged children on the well-meaning North
American adoptive parents without their knowledge or the
support to care for them in the future.

With knowledge comes power. The Children's Aid Society
discloses the birth history of the child. If there is the potential for
problems in the future for this child, support systems can be built
into the adoption agreement that will provide this aid without cost
to the parent in the future. This will not happen if the couple adopt
from overseas.

The process of adopting locally involves a social worker
meeting with the parents, who desire to adopt, to complete a
home study. The study involves the hopes and expectations and
history of the adoptive parents along with references. Once the
home study is complete and the parents are approved to adopt a
child, the social worker will try his or her best to find a child that
best suits the couple's expectations and family dynamics. The
more open-minded the couple is to adopting a child with different
qualities, from a different culture, or a child with possible challenges, the easier and quicker the adoption will be. The more
specific the requirements of the parents the longer it will take. Yet,
it remains, on average, nine months before a child is chosen and
presented to the couple seeking to adopt.

Once a child is available for adoption and the social worker
believes it might be a possible match, the history and picture of
the child will be given to the couple. If they agree that this is the
child they wish to adopt, their name and home study will be
brought to an adoption conference where the child's worker and
the couple's worker will be present to advocate for the child and
the couple. The best interest of the child is always the primary
objective of these meetings. There may be another couple who is

also presented for the purpose of adoption as well. However, due to the very low numbers of people willing to adopt, there often will be only one couple presented.

Once it is agreed that it is in the best interest of the child for the adoption to go forward, the child will begin to have visits with the adoptive parents. Later, papers will be signed, a court date will be set, and the adoption will be finalized.

I understand that not everyone is able either to foster or adopt. There are many other ways that people can make a difference. There are in Canada and the United States foundations and charities that attempt to advocate for the protection of children and are in need of people who are willing to donate either time or money to the cause. The Children's Aid Societies in Canada and the United States both have charitable foundations that work toward supporting the work of child protection and abuse prevention.

Other people have sought to make a difference by making quilts for the babies or by knitting sweaters and booties. These babies very often do not have grandmothers who are able or willing to do these things for them. We have a small but wonderful group of older women who knit and make quilts for each baby that comes through our home. Others have held Teddy Bear auctions and raised money for the foundations or gathered teddy bears and given them to the homes that care for the children.

There are many ways to make a difference. When we choose to do something to make a difference we all enjoy a richer, happier and safer life. You may not be able to open your home either to foster or to adopt children; however, you can support those agencies and people who do that work. And at the very least you can open your heart in other ways that make a difference in the world. Remember, "The only thing that allows evil to flourish is that good people do nothing."

1 www.familyfirst.net/fathersd2000.asp
2 www.newman.baruch.cuny.edu/digital/2001/beecher/lyman.htm
3 Cooper, Bob, *For the Children; 150 Years of Caring for Children and Families,*
   Abbeyfield Publishers, Toronto Ontario, copyright 2001
4 Lela B. Costin, Howard Jacob Karger, David Stoesz, *The Politics of Child Abuse in America,*
   Oxford University Press, copyright 1996, p.51-55
5 Kathleen Kufldt and Brad McKenze, editors, *Child Welfare: Connecting Research,*
   Policy and Practice, Wilfrid Laurier University Press, Waterloo Ontario, Canada, 2003, p.1
6 http://canada.justice.gc.ca/en/ps/fm/childafs.html#factors
7 http://canada.justice.gc.ca/en/ps/fm/childafs.html#factors
8 Kathleen Kufldt and Brad McKenze, editors, *Child Welfare: Connecting Research Policy and*
   Practice, Wilfrid Laurier University Press, Waterloo Ontario, Canada, 2003, p.111-121
9 Ibid, p.274-275
10 Ibid, p.79
11 *Macleans* magazine July 26, 2004, p.20
12 *The National Post,* May 28, 2004, Martin, Sandra, IN3, Money section

Your children are not your children
They are the sons and daughters of life's longing for itself
They come through you but not from you,
And though they are with you yet they belong not to you
You may give them your love but not your thoughts
For they have their own thoughts.
You may house their bodies not their souls.
For their souls dwell in the house of tomorrow,
which you cannot visit, not even in your dreams.
You may strive to be like them, but seek not to make them like
you.
For life goes not backward nor tarries with yesterday.

— *Kahlil Gibran*

ABOUT THE AUTHOR

Prior to becoming a minister in the United Church, John Niles was working in the field of social work. His work took him from treatment homes for the emotionally disturbed child to residential homes for violent and delinquent youth. Later, he worked in a minimum-security halfway house for adults, and completed this phase of his career working in a maximum-security treatment prison for the criminally insane.

John Niles holds numerous degrees in social work, sociology, theology, and psychology. His final degree was a doctorate in psychology. He and his wife Liane have five children and have cared for nearly 1000 others. They are the primary emergency home for all of Metro Toronto. They receive children from birth to five years of age. Many of these children are born addicted to crack and heroin, or suffering from fetal alcohol effects, and/or arrive on their doorstep with broken bones due to abuse.

John and Liane together have been nominated for the Order of Ontario, the Meritorious Service Medal, and the Order of Canada. In 2001 they received the "Community Service Humanitarian of the Year Award" from the Empire Club of Canada. Most recently, they received from the Children's Aid Society the "Heart and Spirit Humanitarian of the Year Award" for 2004.

They have also appeared on CBC Radio, City TV and TVO. Various articles have been written about their work in the *Toronto Star*, *Toronto Sun* and in the *Globe and Mail*, as well as a feature article in the United Church *Observer* magazine.

MESSAGE FROM THE PUBLISHER

In keeping with the tradition established by White Knight Publications, through its authors, of publishing books about social concerns, we are very pleased to have brought to your attention the life that one man and his family live through their service to others: *How I Became Father to 1000 Children and the Lessons I Learned.*

John Niles is an unusual author and a gentle Canadian in almost every way, but when it comes to the defence and improvement of children's rights and services, there is no better champion. Yet, see how he thinks: he writes a book about the *lessons* he has learned from broken and damaged children that he helped to heal through love and respect. Lessons!

What a delight it has been to work with this selfless man who has pledged to be unrelenting in his profession to make society, through his actions and words, into a better child's domain. The growing recognition of his worth is seen in his most recent Humanitarian Award by The Children's Aid Society that he shares with his wife Liane.

White Knight intends to have John Niles as a regular author on the Spring or Fall lists of this publishing house, bringing us issues that must be faced morally, spiritually and with conviction.

Any comments, through our e-mail whitekn@istar.ca or

to our office, that you care to address to Rev. Dr. John Niles or ourselves would be most appreciated. We continue to move into the future to bring solid issues into the light of public scrutiny and challenge.

Bill Belfontaine
Publisher

BOOKS BY WHITE KNIGHT PUBLICATIONS

BIOGRAPHY
- *The Unusual Life and Times of Nancy Ford-Inman*
  – Nancy Erb Kee

GAY ADOPTION
- *A Swim Against The Tide*
  – David R.I. McKinstry

INSPIRATION
- *Conscious Women – Conscious Lives Book 1*
  – Darlene Montgomery
- *Sharing MS (Multiple Sclerosis)*
  – Linda Ironside
- *Sue Kenney's My Camino*
  – Sue Kenney

AVAILABLE SPRING 2005
Conscious Women – Conscious Lives Book 2

Look for your copy in your favourite bookstore!

PERSONAL FINANCES
- *Don't Borrow Money Until You Read This Book*
  – Paul Counter

POETRY
- *Two Voices – A Circle of Love*
  – Serena Williamson Andrew
- *Loveplay*
— Joe Fromstein & Linda Stitt

POLITICS
- *Turning Points* – Ray Argyle

RELATIONSHIP
Books by Dr. K. Sohail and Bette Davis RN MN
- *Love, Sex and Marriage*
- *The Art of Living in Your Green Zone*
- *The Art of Loving in Your Green Zone*
- *The Art of Working in Your Green Zone*

TRUE CRIME – POLICE
- *10-45 Says Death*
  – Kathy McCormack Carter
- *Life on Homicide*
  – Former Toronto Police Chief Bill McCormack
- *The Myth of The Chosen One*
  – Dr. K. Sohail

NEW TOPICS ARE PUBLISHED EVERY SPRING AND FALL

Recommended reading from other publishers

HISTORY
  An Amicable Friendship – Jan Th. J. Krijff
RELIGION
  From Islam to Secular Humanism – Dr. K. Sohail
  Gabriel's Dragon – Arch Priest Fr. Antony Gabriel
  Pro Deo – Prof Ronald M Smith
DREAMS
  Dream Yourself Awake – Darlene Montgomery